A DAY BOOK

By Robert Creeley

A Day Book

Robert Creeley

Charles Scribner's Sons · New York

Grateful acknowledgment is made to the following publications in which some of these poems first appeared: *Best & Co., Britannia, Caterpillar, Elizabeth, Field, Io, Iowa State Liquor Store, Lillabulero, Marijuana Review, Mojo Navigator, New Mexico Quarterly, Paris Review, Partisan Review, Poetry, Stony Brook, The Antioch Review, The New Mexico Review, The World, Transition,* and *Tusitala.*

Acknowledgment is also made to the Alternative Press for its use of "For Betsy and Tom" in its broadside publication *For Betsy and Tom*; to Angel Hair Books for its use of "In London" in its publication *In London*; to the Black Sparrow Press for poems used in *St. Martin's* (in collaboration with Bobbie Creeley); to Bouwerie Editions for their use of "Mary's Fancy" in their publication *Mary's Fancy* and for their use of "For Some Weeks . . . " in their publication *For Some Weeks . . .* (in collaboration with Charles Hinman); to Bouwerie Editions and Edition Domberger for their use of "A Wall" in their publication *A Wall* (in collaboration with William Katz); to Graphis for their use of "A Day Book" in their publication *A Day Book* (in collaboration with R. B. Kitaj); to Portents for their use of "For Benny and Sabina" in their broadside publication *For Benny and Sabina*; and to Shambala and Mudra Publications for their use of "People" in their publication *1.2.3.4.5.6.7.8.9.0* (in collaboration with Arthur Okamura).

Cover by Robert Indiana. Book design and composition at Spring Creek.

for Bobbie

A Day Book   **1**

"To build itself a hideaway high up in the city,
 a room in a tower, timbered with art,
 was all it aimed at, if only it might . . . "
     from *The Riddles*, 29
     translated by Michael Alexander

HE IS WAKING to two particulars. One, that he is to make, before sending it, a copy of the letter, and then realizes the letter has been mailed. And two, that all the assumptions involved in what has happened to himself and his wife, in their so-called fantasy, are literally assumptions. They are not right or wrong. How is the intersection possible? The light is faint in the room. Overhead he makes out the long beams of the ceiling. There seems to them a faint silvery tone, which he reasons is so because they are as the expression goes rough hewn. Light grows slightly in the windows, behind him, just by his head, two slits, then across the room from the bed, a French door with cloth now hanging in front of it. This has a curious yellow tone, as the light increases, and shows the lines of the windows running up and down on either side of the door, which also shows as a series of dark lines, marking its windows.

The descriptions are such that he cannot trust them or rather, would say, fucking is fucking. Having said that, what to say. She lifts her leg. It sounds like a cow. All the tone is wrong. Rather, he can see, behind him, his head magnified, as he turns to look at it, on the white wall close back of him, possibly five times magnified. He raises his hand so that it too appears, darkly but still with the tone of the door, a faint almost powder blue, a lovely hand, four fingers, one thumb. He thinks of the possibilities of fucking. That that part of him, the penis, grows hard, erect, in the dark, he pushes himself onto her, into her. Such dull progress, in the head. Elsewhere in the house as the light increases he hears the sounds of them, wife and children, moving about, faint voices, they are getting ready for school.

The letter leads only to further complications. He will pay the money if required to. The man for whom it is committed is in jail in Mexico. He has never met nor seen him. There is only a somewhat vast emptiness of sentimental assumption to make reason. He had been told of the circumstance weeks ago, slightly, perhaps altogether, drunk, sitting at a table with two younger men who had come to see him, one to interview him for a small local radio station. His so-called, his actual, ego swelled. He saw his head again magnified as the penis now huge he thinks is taken in the hand, then mouth, is sucked in a wetly rhythmic insistence until he feels it, or something in him gathered to a locus, explode, implode, into her face.

Fuck her. Like something lightly in the hand he flips her to the other, in the mind, sees the slight twisting of her body trying to avoid that consequence, then drops to the waiting hands. Always hands, which interrupt, roughly, her gestures, or equally now his own. The man, men, maul her body. He does not want to look nor think of it, but finds himself, in the increasing light, looking. He cannot see, think, clearly what happens. Whatever he thinks of seems to twist away, like a fish turning.

On the wall in front of him a paper he had attached to it, of notices of movies, has loosened at one corner, and now hangs vertically, Science Fiction, Three Cities of Spain. It is all somewhat too linear as if thinking were, he thinks, a line to be followed. Another day will be that one. This one, the new morning of a day.

I KNOW THE CONDITION of those around me, or rather think that I do. One wants to say, *these days*. There is a tacit paranoia I have begun to enter into all such accounting. Again, I do not know if it is an age, my own, biological, or something so patently the case that no one moves apart from it. When Leslie comes he speaks, in his lecture, of the fact, to him, that prose has rejected the self image or the sorrows of Werther kind of fiction. I can feel that sentence just written pacing itself to some argument with him. What will I do without that possibility? But then who cares, in any sense at all. How the head winds itself in the pretension of its own reality.

Actively the words provoke this patter of images. Wind over hollows, so that there is a mutter of sighing voices, something said in some other now past time. Everything this morning, perhaps or almost certainly from the tiredness, has a drifting float to it. Hence write hardly. He picked up the axe and chopped down the tree, which are two of the directions. But if you are in the system, you go out, or out, in. He thinks briefly, is that yin and yang?

But he cannot arouse himself. Nothing stirs, really. In front of him is the Shiva image, the arms so multiple and yet each, in the photograph, of such tactile solidity. The clock is ticking. Ten minutes past seven, and as Alan had noted the night before, the light is viable, changes in the shaded window, to a curious insistent whiteness, and I cannot take hold of things with intention — too vague, too tired to worry.

What I did think of was that I could not really expect it to happen, never quite enough. First love like that. Really the time we were finally lying on the floor of the house, in Maine, way up in Maine on a large island, the girl whose name I forget but will at some point soon remember? Passing in time. Or the imagination of time, or world of whatever creates its experience. He says grandly, we are wound within ourselves, and unwind — that being that. But I do remember the pressure of us then, a straining through our clothing, she flat on the floor and myself on top of her. The he, myself, like a photograph that seems to move floating in air before the other apparent containment, the I. It's all tentative enough. She wants to be fucked. That's what they all want says someone years away, in my ear, kid. Tease them a bit, chew their ear, they'll give it to you. There was a joke of girl at water fountain in factory who bending over to drink finds herself then caught by nipples of each breast by fingers which pinch, twisting them. The sharp, quick flood of wanting. She gasps. But couldn't it be equally, someone else's voice interrupts, it just hurts like hell? That's the joke probably, either way. And for years is sense of, if one does it, that way, the consequence is as stated. These space suits we float in. Gravity keeps us on the same so-called plane, so that the measure of possible presences is the fact we call distance between them. What I always wanted, really, was one of those rigs you put on your back, a sort of jet power pack, like Buck Rogers had, that let him move then at various levels from the ground. Fuck in the air, I say, and that's what Alex uses as climax in all senses, for that novel has the heroine and pilot demon lover fuck as the plane is going into final loop and dive from failure of gas. Fuck anywhere, "now that man has no oar to screw into the earth." Alan is talking of those gods from above, the air, and of the destruction they have made.

EVEN TO GET HERE, I find myself moving letters and other accumulations out of the way, and to have this one sheet of paper, again move paper clips, and again letters out of the way. But why not. One lives as much in that detritus as in some other possibility. Thinking of places I've known wherein there was a most simple order either of poverty or of intent, there was still inevitably that residue — or so I think now, something like the wake of a boat, or echo of sound, smoke vapor.

I was moved, extraordinarily, listening to the journal last night, three pages, that the fellow was reading. He had put it, as he said, in a time capsule when eight years old. Now he was something like twenty. We were sitting in the small room, the so-called 'class' — there was such a feeling, in myself at least, of turgidity, stale feelings, either intensely programmatic as my own had become in the attempt to make something clear, or else just baffled. I watched the eyes of the girl across from me on the couch, trying to see what she was feeling beyond the mask of her makeup. The body was at least attentive, one thought. The journal was literally a small spiral-ring notebook. He said his family had given him one each Christmas. The writing began with a boy who immediately became a girl who in turn then qualified the boy, and the sex moved back and forth in that identity. I had been trying to make clear that words might be lived in, in this way, and now he had, unexpectedly, "off the subject," as he said, given me my demonstration. Pre-pubescent, we thought. Yet the sexual was very insistent — and in this play of *he* and *she*, I was also exploring the change, now woman, now man.

Outside Spot barking, the morning shifting again through the oblique window I can see to my right. To the left, the square of light in the door, covered by the red cloth. The watch, hung on a nail, makes a lovely deliberate ticking. Looking then at the small post card of Shelley "By Amelia Curran, 1819" which was painted, then, three years before his death, I can make nothing of it — no sense clear of who he is in the image. He holds, hieratically, a feather quill pen in his right hand. The face seems utterly opaque except for something about the eyes and the curiously firm set of the mouth in an intent he is feeling, a way of being there. Allen's sense of writing as a time capsule. The myriad deaths and births, the systems exploding, going out, sending the fading messages, the space sea of times and places.

Mrs. Gutierrez, come to get the wash yesterday, sitting at the kitchen table, describes what the doctor has told her of stroke, to wit, fat people — her own problem being overweight — don't die, they have strokes, and then their own people don't want to have to do with them. Once or twice, perhaps, but then the smell, the condition, repels them. She doesn't say it like that, but I do. She speaks in a quick heavy manner of accent. But the picture, so to speak, of such an almost delightful obesity, sunk in sloth, like they say, stricken, the wandering eyes, speechless, "going out," as the related turn away in repulsion. Also a note in the paper of a few days ago apropos a doctor's report of what he considers the fact of a biological information of death in the system previous to its consciousness — roughly a year previous. We seem to live in one, scattered by the particular occasion, and spend so-called life attempting to recover coherence. The parts of a body, the chapters of a book.

THIS TIME, NIGHT. Some sense obviously of when does the story start, or more, what point the going on and on. I can do that, i.e., know it can be an exercise I simply continue till I'm either altogether bored with it, or have to assume it can't come to more than such boredom. But what's the other side — not what had earlier been attractive in Olson's use of Rimbaud's, "the other side of despair" — which *is* the drama, somehow, immediately, but not what this is involved with, somehow.

Night, now, or day, now, or ten o'clock in the morning, or at night, or some time whitely between, or there. Or here. Where else would it be. Alan's: now here/ nowhere.

But you are here. Say it that way. Drawing the face in. So that the mouth, like the Cheshire cat's, appears. So that a sudden slap obviously makes you wince, and wonder why there should be such sudden anger at your appearance. Where have you been. No need, really, to explain. If you thought to, you would have, and myself would also appear, provided with that summons. We can surely see the two of us sitting, now that the initial discomfort is past, all that left behind, and what fears or confusions either one of us might have been feeling would be done with too.

Twenty past twelve midnight. The girls just returned home from the school carnival, delayed by Mr. Muench's having tried to try out a bongo board, apparently has slipped in the process, and hurt himself.

"There's a bongo board you know? Mr. Muench fell off it, and bruised his ribs." Kate gets ready for bed. Hear sounds of her taking off sweater, rest of clothing. The cat's in there somewhere. It's late. It's been a long day. I took Alan with me up to Taos to bring Sascha the plastic for the windows of his house. We don't see Sascha, but it's a pleasure to see where he is living, small house south down a valley, facing from the west side, the length of the Sangre de Cristos. Brook runs along the road. Lovely brilliant glitter of sun on the water. Lovely sounds, wetness. Opening fence, walking up field to his house, there is a flock of sheep, then a few cows, and horse. Try to think of when young, seventeen as he is. Alan says, not that again. Me too, I guess. But what a lovely place to think of, be at, at that age, or possibly only idealism of not being there, nor that age. But the sun is so yellow, so slanting across the fields. Kids coming home from school, I watch one hoist himself over the fence, to cross short field to his yard. Another, about seven, looks up as I wave and waves back. There is a lovely brilliant clarity to the air, all the detail of the mountains very distinct, and also, the closer edges of the trees. We follow the dirt road back, cross over the bridge, past the store and on the porch a girl Alan has spoken of noticing on the way is still there, with her boy now, leaning toward him. I see them kiss.

What one wants, after tiredness, after all the day of driving, some nostalgia of such kind. When I was young, like they say. I thought, seeing the water of that brook, of New Hampshire brooks. But it was really in Massachusetts. Alan says, like Vermont, and continues to tell me of going skiing with first wife in Vermont, how he loved it, the place and tone of people, the aunt who was really not related but would come for divers family festivities like Christmas.

EIGHT DAYS LATER. Which seems incredible, like, just a moment ago it was I was sitting here, but it's morning, like they say, about seven, and Bobbie's gone back to bed. Then the old friend's arrival and my own sense we do get older, just by virtue of the juxtaposition, chum. Two old gaffers chatting. Or rather — a curiously abstract tone given to anything we say by the drifting vagueness of his junkie-ism. I want to warm him, or reach him. It's a sentimental insistence I have as habit, but don't longer feel as meaning much. Nor does he really need it. That's what I think then.

But the eight days absent, gone through, now more to the point.

It's night. Then it *was* morning, when I was writing here, at the same table, same Shelley-face, Shiva. What is that space comes between. It becomes for the time impossible to put in that place an actual time passage. Only bits and pieces, e.g., the apparently broken nose I now have, Alan's leaving, Ed's arrival with his girl, the flu, the car's not starting day after day. Like the old business of notches on a stick, or rows of *x*'s. Accounting for it.

You won't pay half though, not what you've spent. You couldn't begin to. You might now want to settle accounts but after all you've done, you'd be another lifetime paying. And paying — and paying. That's a sense of proper delight makes the mind warm to its work. It would do better to simply rage when able, and be quiet for the rest, than pay it back to where it never damn well came from. So I say, or think to.

Fucking visitors anyhow. Ed says, are we bothering you — at point I feel so literally sick I could vomit on him, and know the question, in my Machiavellian yet fever, is only to reassure him. Is it hurting you, love. Do you mind I ate the last of the meat. Are you sure you've no use for it. Fuck 'em. I am a proper beast when ill and what the hell else should I be. For once the body dictates, and the only problem is not to stay ill, for the sheer delight of that fact. As, for example, that lovely part, was it, in Mann, *The Magic Mountain*, wanting to spit on the unsick so as to convert them. There is such malice in a little edge of sickness, that is, when one's not sick enough just to whimper, but feels the particular shift from 'normal' to 'ill' just enough to place the difference, and therefore have use of it.

There was one lovely night of sheer drunkenness, beyond anger happily, so the body floated in its own roundness, and stand or fall, it was all one. The next morning I was bruised from head to foot, including the nose, but such a relief, so much had got backed up on Alan's own restlessness and confusions, and the talking so unremittingly of goddamn zen and goddamn revolution, and nothing *here*, or just literally *what* one could put one's hand on. I had to wait till I was drunk, to let it out — and then it came out sans some sneer against him. Which was not the point, at all. He is as painfully about his life as anyone I might think of — which is or is not the point.

Fading a little. Can't reach it, in time. Over that way, or this way. Was it there, etc. You can't remember anymore nor is there much reason to. It'll be by again, if intended to. It's all a plan somehow, or they'll tell us. Lovely to think there's an occasion more than what you think. To eat and sleep.

DRIVEN TO IT, not by need of some external kind, but rather because he wanted to, or thought he did — to *see* something, be witness to it, yet not possible to see in that, he could propose at least, it did not exist. That sense of, how do I know what I'm going to say before I've said it, a convenience at best surely for what might be as little known after said, as before. But there at least. He wasn't really interested in that fact at all. What was there, or would be. More problems, if it were then up to him either to defend or to justify. He simply liked the fact of writing, both in doing it and as it then became, in the intimacy still possible at that moment, something just done and not as yet involved with other possible questions.

Formalist, he found himself straightening the rug, dumping ashtrays, insistently checking his experience of the room, rooms, to see if the familiar order were continuingly the case. But otherwise had also impulse or something made him jump when no chance of landing anywhere seemed likely.

But the girl said, *practical* of him — almost a threat, he felt. She was instantly attractive, crazy long body, great energy in it, black, but literally brown, or in fact such words, of color, were not at all the fact of skin. *We all wear leather*, said Ed Dorn, *i.e., skin*. She was lovely, briefly to be there. One of those people one finds oneself looking at so openly there is almost a wince, one's own, at what an intimacy has been recognized. She was, I suppose, womanly just that she took such fact very happily, and wasn't in the least put off or if so, looked simply about her with a womanly, and slight, confusion. But the "practical" stuck somehow, she said it so wisely, next morning before they were off again, enroute to San Francisco, for the first time west, both herself and the other girl, with his own friend John like a weirdly wise tourguide. It was his car but the ladies were providing money for the gas, etc. Some of the first conversation had been about the way the money went. Her eyes were particularly love-ly, very direct, very warm, so that the head seemed somehow to pull back from them, like hair pulled back, as at times hers was, to make even more emphasized the center her eyes were, in her face. Yet "practical"—making the edge between so-called Taurus and so-called Gemini, his own situation, on the "cusp," someone had told him — perhaps his mother since he could now hear her voice in his head saying that final "sp" (ss-peh, but not sepa-rated, just said *clearly*) — making that sense of Taurus, its fine dependable dogged dreariness, "practical," seem even more what he was than he'd dared to fear. By day a mild schizophrenic, by night a tireless pragmatist.

He wanted to fuck his wife all the time now. Yet having done so, would have his head fill with 'things to do,' almost lists of them, as if the relief of coming, like they say — and though understandable, it's an odd phrase finally to mean the emission of semen, but must mean something like, *it's me, I'm here!*, whereas 'emission' would have the slightly military sense of, that which has been sent forth . . . . As if the relief of coming cleared the way back into one's self, and the world, of the particular, not the imagined, thereby vanished till it recurred again in the need either to find place to piss or place one's member elsewise, in the act of love. Or eat, or sleep, or whatever all that was constitutes bodily needs and functions. Did one fuck more in the fear of fucking less. Possibly. But there had never been the experience of great bounding leaps of frustration. At best, deep comfort. At worst, the inappropriate, and hence the lack of a place to be. Betimes — so-called wet dreams or else masturbation. In such wise had days and nights been passed.

WHAT DOESN'T SATISFY is what had, at the outset, seemed the specific permission possible. Say anything, i.e., shit, fuck, cunt, etc. In my own head these words are now so much a faded condition, in themselves, no energy seems to come from them. You have to have them somewhere, not placed, but met — in the literal *cunt*, the legs now open to expose it. Or coming home, the *catshit* on the rug with its almost acrid smell. Or *fuck you*, he says, daring what he hopes will be the reaction, so that he is freed to club me.

Not one without the other, nothing else in the fading sea, with whatever winds move its surface. So that what had seemed the utterly placid surface, glassy, as they say, becomes otherwise. I remember one time in teaching, at that point Latin to a group of eighth graders, there was always an almost attractive whispering as I'd come into the room, like leaves rustling, but with sudden quick bursts of sharper sounds, giggling, or the high-pitched blurt of just those words I had thought, at my age, to have use of. At first I paid no attention, depending on that sense of it, that it would go away by itself once the interest had been exhausted. But, witness myself, the interest doesn't exhaust itself. There grows a habit, so to speak, of the possibility and power which the words possess. But now I remember her, the first woman I ever did, saying, almost in hysteria, *fuck* me — *Do* it. It's the one time the word does stay in my head, forever. But now, with the giggling, impatient just to get them settled enough to begin with the day's work, and so be that much the sooner rid of it, what can I do. I get up, look at them, then go to the board while they continue, paying me only covert attention, and then write on it as quickly and with as large letters as I can manage, *SHIT!* They all grow immediately silent, some blush, and so I say to them in that convenience I think mistakenly given to adults, *shit.* That is the word. Are there any others you would like to consider? And continue then with some vague lecture on 'power' words, and how of course we all make use of them, and are also, equally, attracted to them.

But that other time, in the fumbling, despairing fact of its demand — the word was as fierce as an axe, and as practical. And as deeply the mystery she was as I could ever find other sense of. It seems to me at times as if, at the center of all that these women are, and that literal mystery to which they invite me, or Homer was a fucking idiot with his Circe, and she more full of shit than even Odysseus — the dumb cunt .... No, but a quiet almost murmured babble, so that you have to come closer, and listen hard, to catch in the mumbling, and in even the incredibly ugly and aged face pushed at you, with all that repulsion of broken teeth and hairs growing out of moles and foul, hissing breath and bleared obscene eyes, *those words*. And love it, incredibly *her*, as she transforms into that imagined delight you had held of her so long before the sight of her actual fact. She delights, you are held in the succulent wonder, fondled, teased, and just those words come whispering into your ear.

I had read somewhere that men are much more apt to engage in sexual activity with an image, a fantasy, in their heads, than are women. Perhaps that relates to their fact as form-makers, whatever finally that comes to — but also true seems the other fact I have been held by at least, that women are source, are the material condition. I avoid my pompous intent by giving over all arbitration, by anyone, or argument. Laughing, the proof is in the pudding. One reason I have not been attracted sexually to animals is possibly because they cannot speak. I hear that incredible lore, in those words, echoing, remembering all there ever was or ever could be of any of it.

EVEN TO BEGIN to say this takes extraordinary care, i.e., the paper gets jammed, the wrong key gets punched, and what literally *is* to be said gets as adamant as the timetable for an eastern railroad, or the seating arrangements at some unimaginable ball. And what *is*, to be said: Today — to mark it — I came into the waiting room of the dentist's office where my two daughters (the two still at home) had been brought, with Bobbie, my wife, to have their teeth cleaned. (But like some horrible pun I find myself typing, probably drunk, 'teetch' for 'teeth' — even *now* having to erase the horrid *c . . . .*) I had been to the airport, after leaving them there, I felt shocked, had neither eaten nor done more than dress, after an elaborate shower and so on, getting myself dressed to teach, though it seemed as though the sun could scarcely have risen, and all had a sluggish sullen air to it. God knows the children no more interested (were) in the getting cleaned (teeth) than me in getting them (there).

All like that. Inertia, difficulty, resentment. Sullen, silent, opaque and consistently resistant, the whole damn day a sort of tribunal of impossibilities. Like some idiot, though graced with an acceptance, his own and the idiot Department's (English), of his own qualifications as a so-called Ph.D.

I had been to the airport, to get a ticket for a flight (not to anywhere by any instinct), and all having gone well, drove, happily without incident, to where I had left them all. I went into the waiting room — in brick building coincident with jail, courthouse, school, factory, store, as Mailer intelligently insists — and saw two people sitting, and could not recognize any, in that curious dimness such places have, for my own view of things. Was, of course, instantly paranoid, expecting, hoping, to be identified momently by them so as to have *place* there, too. So *saw* a young woman, pleasant in appearance, sitting to the left, with legs crossed, attractive, and a lovely fall of brown hair, absorbed, as they say, in a magazine. And across from her, one of those inevitable bitches of the late forties (her own age) who 'checks out,' as the expression is, any *late* arrival to her own environs, whether same be a garbage pail or the Ritz. So felt therefore instant displacement and paranoia, and looked desperately for any sign of the three people I had brought there some half hour before. The so-called problem with doctors' or dentists' offices, as jails, is, *where* are people in them. Not to mention, *in* what circumstance.

So now, *where* — were they. Not to panic, I walked over to a shelf, rack, of magazines, and began to look through them, and then looking, covertly, at the girl sitting to the left, with that lovely hair, saw she was literally my daughter Sarah. Who had, she said, been so absorbed simply to avoid the engagement of the bitch, the soured and vicious person (I stake my life on such assumptions), was sitting across the room from her.

What *is* to say, is, this day, I give testament to my daughter's having entered that opaque state, for me, god knows male, of whatever it is, is womanhood. I did not recognize her, but saw, instead, a young woman of viable and attractive form — and liked her, and wanted therefore to know more of her. In short, a momentous day — to be swept clean of idiot distraction, persons, the dead student, the vicious elder woman, the timetable, the clutter — to be clearly, Sarah, age eleven, *is* a woman.

HAD DRIVEN DOWN to Bernalillo, in the valley below us here — we are up in a small town, Placitas, at the north end of the Sandia Mountains, in the foothills, about 7000 feet — to mail letters, restless, about two in the afternoon, with Bobbie and the girls having gone into Albuquerque, etc. Flat sort of chilled afternoon. High, faint sun, which as I turn off the highway into the mainstreet of Bernalillo, sits directly in front of me. The street here is wide, very western in look now since a few years ago what had been the store fronts and look of various houses along it were cut back to permit the widening of the road. It's predominantly Mexican, and is used also by the Pueblo Indians —

Sandia, Santa Ana, Zia, San Felipe, et al. Just about as I get to the highschool, on the right, I suddenly confront a parade coming up the other side of the street towards me, led by one of the town's police cars, with that heavy anonymous-looking dark glasses policeman, smiling, happily, with, behind him, about four abreast and some six to eight deep in rows, horsemen, with yellow flashes on their right sleeves I can not read — Sheriff's Posse? — and god knows authentic in appearance, of various ages, all predominantly Mexican, young and old, with those about in their thirties, say, very conscious of their style and riding with a very upright, almost fierce sort of pride. I pull over to the right and stop completely, Spot back of me on the seat, panting, so I roll down the window, and watch, and listen, as the parade goes on past me to the left. So now simply the notes thereof: Parade — first police car; horses & men; firetruck (this is local and from time to time sounds its siren, as does the police car); drum majorettes (Mexican again — with the same style as the riders, very conscious somehow, or else in that reputed sense, *sleepy*, drowsing almost in the movement); band number one: red tunics, grey pants — (this is) Bernalillo High School Band; (then) four cars, then float — yellow and light blue — CUBA HIGH SCHOOL RAMS (which then explains the occasion, i.e., it must be two teams are playing against each other, basketball? hardly anything else on January 17, 1969) — with their band — dark blue and gold. High faint sun — from head of street. Spot pants back of me. Floats then numbered (1,2,3,4, etc.) — Frank's Conoco — etc. "Put a bear in your pot" (referring to Bernalillo).

I turn off finally onto a dirt road runs back of the town, off to the west mesa, the houses moving back toward it, all one story, mostly adobe, or else cement block, and to the left, the east, about five or six miles distant, the bulk of the Sandias like a section of the earth has lifted, broken clear, and raised up on edge. Then turn back toward the main street, having driven parallel to it for a while, coming out just below the post office, in the one block of businesses, so turn back toward it, go in, am greeted by the post office official, like they say, who asks me, am I still living in Placitas, after I've mentioned the parade, and says he is going to run for the school board, and will be up to see us. I demur, in a way, saying my wife has much interest, which she had had but I question if she continues to. Going out, drive then back up the street, back of the parade, and at one point come abreast of it, in the left lane, realizing it is making an about-turn opposite the highschool, so stop there back of a car to wait for the street to clear — as floats, people, go by now on both sides. Slogans on floats like, Flush the Bears! (on float with teddy bear, purple and white, on toilet) or Stone the Bears! (with kids sitting in car with big display bottles of whiskey) — and against the wire mesh of the highschool fence, kids on the inside watching, in a lovely delight.

ALL THE DAY has seemed echo after echo of previous condition — in whatever person or sense of person was ever real in it. I don't know any longer what actually is the proposal but for some hopefully initial sense of who was there, literally, and what I felt myself to have to do with them. I am speaking of children — the first child and son ever born to me, for one, and his brother, and sister. What a curious rhetoric seems to come even in saying it. But now, knowing even if briefly the latter two, humanly there is for me at least such persistent resonance in that relation. I don't want to make them subject to my own feelings, nor do I really think that will be the occasion in any case.

But such damned echoes . . . . Speaking to their mother this morning on the phone, cross-country like they say, from a place I feel myself almost literally to have earned, a life with people I love and who love me — all that cagey, double edge of statement is so insistently distasteful, all that dull 'I know better' that comes in her voice, and the almost shocked manner of the child-like 'saying of the piece' — what is it makes it be so.

I've been trying to know what it is to be specifically myself in this point of age, almost asking people how they are feeling in it, as one would fellow travelers in some situation, shipwreck or great happiness, possibly. Such confoundings of myself, in the past, are seemingly now absent. Fears, ways of stating oneself, and so on, do seem truly to have taken themselves off. I don't think it's a question really of having done anything, though I've reassured myself of that fact, perhaps more in teaching than in writing — or in the last there is no point of rest permits one to feel at rest with, 'there, I've done it, and that's that.' Curious that Benjamin DeMott this morning on the phone should say, I hear you're the hero now — or so-called words to that effect, but sans some convenient self-demurring, or whatever, I could answer, I'm not — very much to him, who would know, I think, the incredible deadness inherent in any term of that assumption. Straight forward, is forever the only way.

And whereas now these dilemmas of how to be of use to these people, hardly though still inevitably children, hopefully in some sense of mine,— all the rest of such facts as one calls 'human relations,' all these so densely apparent, almost daily, and so changingly and variously open, adamantly so it would seem. Think, though no sophistication, two days ago one was entering, by a process of self-reality like either a huge sky or else an incredibly absolute tunnel, the possibility of that woman one called 'wife's' fucking a randomly met though pleasant man. 'Why not' would prove the social history of our so-called age, but the literal possibility, in fact, like they say, would prove the alternate truth of human condition. No one owns. I think the most useful truth I've been given to acknowledge of others, as a man, is that in one's own experience another's is not necessarily denied nor increased. Years ago now, remembering that situation of separating from that first wife, Olson's parallel, in his own confusions, put as he said, that one could love *two* — or myriad, as I now find, either in myself or in another, and the relation to *one* is not of that fact lost. Will it be that someday we come to some relation with those who make up our condition, *humans*, that will not argue their histories as all that they depend upon for relation — or else, more accurately, that what they do is more relevant to all their lives, one by one or all in all, than what they didn't. I feel such trust in life, once I stop all that previous qualification — just that I know I'm alive, and witness it with such pleasure in others, *we are here* — I'm happy, in the most simplistic of senses. I've thought a lot, like they say, but more than that I've not found.

I MUST NOW FATHOM an old judgment which, I believe, is but one of Condillac's ideas: it was that it's useless to read books of logic; it's essential to try to reason correctly, and that's all.

The rules that Tracy prescribes at the end of his *Science de Nos Moyens de Connaître* are so simple that I can quite well try to put them into practice. They consist in retracing the memory of the thing on which one wishes to reason, and then in being careful to see that the subject always contains the attribute given it.

But this happy temporary release from cares and troubles I enjoyed but a few moments, when I was awakened and greatly surprised by the terrifying screams of owls in the deep swamps around me; and what increased my extreme misery was the difficulty of getting quite awake; and yet hearing at the same time such screaming and shouting which increased and spread every way for miles around, in dreadful peals vibrating through the dark extensive forests, meadows, and lakes. I could not after this surprise recover my former peaceable state and tranquillity of mind and repose, during the long night; and I believe it was happy for me that I was awakened, for at that moment the crocodile was dashing my canoe against the roots of the tree, endeavouring to get into her for the fish, which I however prevented.

Even here though I myself am pursuing the same instinctive course as the veriest human animal you can think of — I am however young [old] writing at random — straining at particles of light in the midst of a great darkness — without knowing the bearing of any one assertion of any one opinion. Yet may I not be in this free from sin? May there not be superior beings amused with any graceful, though instinctive attitude my mind may fall into, as I am entertained with the alertness of a stoat or the anxiety of a deer? Though a quarrel in the streets is a thing to be hated, the energies displayed in it are fine; the commonest man shows a grace in his quarrel. By a superior being our reasonings may take the same tone — though erroneous they may be fine. This is the very thing in which consists poetry; and if so it is not so fine a thing as philosophy — for the same reason that an eagle is not so fine a thing as a truth. Give me this credit. Do you not think I strive — to know myself?

Finding then everything in due tone and order, I remembered my fears, only to make a jest of them to myself. And now, palpably mistress of any size of man, and triumphing in my double achievement of pleasure and revenge, I abandoned myself entirely to the ideas of all the delight I had swam in. I lay stretching out, glowingly alive all over, and tossing with a burning impatience for the renewal of joys that had sinned but in a sweet excess; nor did I lose my longing, for about ten in the morning, according to expectation, Will, my new humble sweetheart, came with a message from his Master, Mr. H., to know how I did. I had taken care to send my maid on an errand into the city, that I was sure would take up time enough; and, from the people of the house, I had nothing to fear, as they were plain good sort of folks, and wise enough to mind no other people's business than they could well help.

One path only is left for us to speak of, namely, that *It is*. In this path are very many tokens that what is is uncreated and indestructible; for it is complete, immoveable, and without end. Nor was it ever, nor will it be; for now *it is*, all at once, a continuous one.

SHE WAS LOVELY, then, in the darkness. Tired, but with that sweet tone of an almost playful if protesting abandon, *not to now*, as one says. What had he been thinking? Simply that, sitting at the table in the kitchen with the friend, literally, the other man, it was inextricably time to know a fact. In his own response to her, or hers to him, they were so entangled in their own feelings, and if she became object to him, then by that he had withdrawn from her, so as to know her more clearly. She could not be in that the specific woman she was.

So now he came in, with the other still in the hall back of him, or perhaps he had not left the kitchen as yet. That was it. The other man was still back there, in the outer room, possibly as displaced, but eager, as he was, turning on the light, so that she turned sleepily around and looked up, smiling, I think, with that moist soft tone of muzziness. His cock was already hard, excited by even what he was saying, that he wanted to fuck her with the other, or really the other way round, and when he had gone to get the other man, reassuring her, who was aroused also, that it would be all right, both took off their clothes, as she had, lying with sharply white body, red and white and black, her hair, with the bedclothes pulled off, and as they both in an awkwardness moved toward her, she eased them by smiling, and reached to take the other against her, so that he now took position beside them, back of her, reaching over the arch of her back to stroke her tits, as the other was now down on her, sucking, the cunt, as she moved against him, making soft sweet moans, as one says, and became, before him, the two, her incredible whiteness, smaller in body literally than he had known, and now the man on her, sucking, as she pushed against him and shuddered. They clung together. He, back of them, had fallen into a curious object of his own, as if he were looking in a window, a long space, but her hand came back of her to feel his cock, then as the man seized her harder, locked again with him, arched and fucking in completed intensity.

There was another moment, somewhere in the time, he lay by her buttocks, stroking, as she had knelt over the other to take his cock in her mouth, with both hands cupped over it, below her mouth, with the lips extended around it, and hair falling over his stomach, up and down, with quick sudden intensity, the man up then pushing, to go *ahhh*, and come.

Later, it was already faint morning, at the windows, the long french door, the man and the woman with him were kneeling nude on the floor before them as they now themselves fucked slowly, lazily, on the bed. He was fucking her from the back, his cock up the crotch of her legs to her cunt and his fingers rubbing her clitoris. The two in front of them, hierarchically, slowly, made love. The woman sucked the man's cock, up and down, slowly, the mouth moving back and forth, and the long hair falling, the body almost stern in its concentration. He had placed both hands on her shoulders and drew her back and forth as she at times stroked his cock, or else placed her hands on his hips. Slowly, almost gravely, it went on, while on the bed, he watched, felt his own cock tense with it, could not see the eyes facing also toward the sight, hers, erotic, lovely, tight with interest, his own, fucking, fucking in knowledge of animals, in delight and permission of animals, gravely, sweetly, humans without fear or jealousy, but intensive increasing provocation. So that now, in dreams as it were, he unclothed her, beckoned them forward, saw their own clothes fall, the cocks stiff, engaged them with her, one after one after one.

PIVOTS UPON EVERYTHING, that business if you don't see it now, you'll never have another chance. Like bagels, bacon, bedpost rhymes with b, or else the rhythm does, uncle, irish, or offens(ive). You play with it. His broke soon after he got it. That Christmas. That night.

Sweating profusely. He profuses to be a teacher of the young. He is tired. He is sitting in a room facing wall some twenty miles from Chicago. White tired. It's getting close to six o'clock and the shops will be closing, the people coming home. A memory of white streets, freshly fallen snow, the light catches in a lovely glow around it, somehow the sense of aureole, apart from aura, a halo of roses, green dreams but none so dominant it makes a sense to get home to.

Small animals in well contrived cage, of glass, with open top the very pleasant orange brown dog, a mut, looks down into but does not touch. Kangaroo mouses, seem bright, fresh, at least pleasing to human attention and valuation insofar as same in the system admitting them, and/or has brought them, from Tibet, or Mongolia, or any name you want to, to make them hear. One jumps into revolving wire cage, making it spin round, and by clasping its belly to the ladderlike interstices, goes round and round, rightside up upside down, and then in a particularly attractive way, flips out, at the top of the spin, and somehow lands rightside up.

Students, viz., those who study in this case, but more, a present social condition of person, those who are, at these institutions of various size and density, and talking, talking, we all talk, the first time I was seen hereabouts, but had slipped in, when he was looking, I wasn't, came in the only way you get in, by just opening the so-called door.

He can't make heads nor tails of this, he can't. Nor can I. What was he saying, i.e., no sooner had he said it, I was thinking, that's a pretty glib assumption, for such a serious man who says he is. No but I think what's actually on his mind is some filling of paper, like he wants to, like dinner he can't eat, but asked for. You said you were hungry. Or in love. Or tired. Or many things indeed, and now you're stuck with it. Try climbing out of that skin by your neat little agencies. Or get a computer remembers that, for one thing — you said you were tired. You don't resolve the argument that way. So hits him, full in the face, such a delicious relaxation after all these years of disappointment, really, in what were the endless expectations, better job, at least more pertinent to his background and actual experience, not to mention what, underneath, he was really feeling. Say, for example, that he is employed to eat shit in the subway. One, you don't find much. Two, it tastes bad. Or good. It's the same, and/or what they call, or used to call, or perhaps even did call, when I is or was a boy, since you don't know what I is except as you says so. That wasn't any job any man ever had in any case. But it was shit sure enough. You could smell it on him, not a smell easily removed. You speaks metaphorically? Quick perception of the relation between things, hallmark of genius — and didn't have to think it, just wrote it, baby, just damn well wrote it.

So the old girl must be out she don't answer phone, and probably tired of hearing it all in any case. Lord love a duck, go fuck a tiger. But he really wants to go home he says. Must have been awful, on those moors, hearing those people about to be used in horrible sex acts, just children, saying, I wants to go home. Not funny, old sport. No laugh when you find yourself gone, down the drain, just flushed with the end of it. Dirty trickle, that's all. Now the drain's stopped, and there will not be another this evening. Crazy trail end of smoke, like there used to be, down the tracks, through Acton, when he was a kid, and over that intervale and river, going to sleep or trying to, would come sound of, chuff, chuff, chuff. Whoo, whoo.

IN THE BOAT OF IT, so to speak, going, but rather in the fact that from *here* is *there*, and the past a wake of curious resonance, and forward no more than the body's movement, in walking, the one foot lifting, to find place ahead of itself, else behind.

So that, at times, there are experiences, suppose them, of oneself, or whatever it is does manage the containment, at least so experienced, and nothing falls in or out of it but fluids, effluvia, spit, shit, little flakes of dried skin, and occasional 'parts' lost for a variety of reasons, and also the whole bulk of words constituting, also, actions, as if one hit the future, saw the stone skip a myriad number of times, light dazzle, on the water's surface, and then, as the boat continues, looks back, as they say, to see the stone disappear. Words. Such a lovely particular abstraction, torn out of whatever else can be felt as coincident. 'I can't find the right words . . . . ' Or, in no possession thereof, but now insistently possessed of them, choked, stuffed, spills out all the possibilities, of there being, one, no reason, two, all reason, three, rage, four, confusion, five, pain, six, pleasure, seven, *use* certainly, eight, a possibility, nine, delight in any *material* condition, and zero, or ten, put the one in front of it, and return thereto — one can suppose them then to enter the room, probably the bedroom (bathroom?), him screaming hers, her's, substance, in him. A curious twist on all occasion.

So that — there is a curious mirror, when one reflects the other, and in that, other sees not one, but other as one. 'Be neat, speak courteously, make a good impression' — and hence the false face carried so persistently front of what might be seen, and must be. What else to look at. But surely there is a relief in that intention, if any has any possibility. Oh, so sorry. Here, take this chair. Yes, it probably will rain.

But — "It was funny. You went in and out, like, you weren't

what I supposed you would be. You were simply talking. At the luncheon, for example. But when you read, it was both you, that way, then I saw you with almost an aura, all around you like a very large halo, Olson, Duncan, Ginsberg . . . . " Or words to that effect. Something like that said. It was so late, dark, nothing really very clear in hearing it. Such a lovely solid body somehow. Attractive. Really, in that basic sense, drawing to itself the alternate energy. Not me really, one thought. Real — it's a different thing, of course. Gets tired, older, certainly, but is *here* — has only itself to be in. Can't be image only of some other experience of it.

When you were young . . . . When one was young, it becomes a memory to say so. It is another image, nostalgia perhaps. But she says, don't talk about *age*. Such an interesting subject, though. Williams — "You reach for it, you feel the impulse, your mind is sharp enough, but when you reach, your fingers can't articulate, you can't keep up with the impulse, you *want* to, but it all fails you, won't work . . . . " He certainly didn't like it. But others — possibly. He said, it's supposed to be a fruition, the accumulation and success, most hopefully, of all you've intended — the time you can decently rest from it, see what's become of what you've meant to do, and, having, as one's wont to say, succeeded, enjoy it. Decently earned rest from it. But it's not like that. You reach for it, you feel the impulse, your mind is sharp enough, but when you reach, your fingers can't articulate, you can't keep up with the impulse, you *want* to, but it all fails you, won't work . . . .

Someone was speaking of the elderly lady who, looking in the mirror, saw the face she couldn't accept as hers, all the wrinkles, the change in it, in that *inside* she was a girl still. *Me* . . .

Unacceptable, that the mountain can break up, the sea diminish? How is that possible. Ah. All one's life one was alive! Do you think they're happy up there? Where. Oh, wherever they are now. Who knows. What? Oh, whether or not they are. Well, not for us to think of. We're here.

ENTHUSIASMS, THE ENERGIES that come therefrom—like, 'My heart leaps up when I behold . . . ' With such insistent fact. Wondering if one's response, to the younger man, is possibly just a way to experience this state, so lovely, fresh, renewing, in its possibility. And not, or then again perhaps, some unrecognized edge of homosexual content in oneself. But that too, acknowledged. So beautiful they really are, at just that moment of so-called age all is poised on the possibility, and their own energies are so moving.

Coming out of the postoffice, the town so curious or not at all so in its rather insistent, comfortable and apparent wealth — like the lovely time Duncan, in the house of the pleasantly wealthy woman, is saying in that high-pitched excitement of his, "Money, money, money! I can almost smell it!" — anyhow that tone, and the lady following behind suddenly says, "Are you *English?*" — meaning apparently the tones of the conversation she is overhearing, and says, "Suddenly I thought we were back in London! You know, we just came from there," herself unequivocally American and the answer is, no, *New* England, and now living in *New* Mexico, and very *much* American. And so forth.

A bright sunlit day — after a long time, it seems, of rain, snow, fog, a chill in all the air. The vagueness, in that sense, of the hotel room now shifts to a particularity, and one is *at home,* knows where the things familiar to oneself are, moves in the space with pleasure and interest, familiarly. Like John Cage's saying, why not a motel, and what else does one need — and surely for those who live primarily in their own condition, almost a skin not to absent from nor could one be, the place of the body is the place one lives in, and the mind follows and makes do. But — as Olson — that fact of *habits* and *haunts,* so hardly earned in a way, and found. As New England — odors, sounds, senses of wetness, ways streets move, trees, the movement of the ground, senses of distance, smells, tones of voices, light. One wants to, at last, *be there* beyond the intention in all senses, simply there.

Faded, dulled? Not really. *Elsewhere* in one's self, another part, as one might say, another function possibly — if life, whatever it is, can be so divided into contents. Chapter one, head, chapter two, heart, etc. Who knows — but it can't be a discretion, whatever it is. But what had happened to love, so to speak — when its person is absent. Desire continues, but cannot find its response. Or rather turns to other terms of it, talking, talking, talking, talking — god knows a deluge of it, and when the young man comes up to the room, almost a shyness one feels, it is so curiously intimate, so flooded with a privileged meaning.

So anyhow. Who is it out there, oneself, looking at oneself, from within. The mirror. Real because it is there? The man who looks in the mirror and sees no image of himself reflected? Lost in time and space? Etc. Or Narcissus, kneeling, sees the wavering beauty, the body of his own life, there reflected.

Aunt Bernice — in trailer with Mother, crunky, derelict somehow trailer park, Nokomis, Florida, Route something or other, at the scrub edge of the town, within which an almost terrifying institutional-like boys' school, military. And the sea there is a bay, a salt lake — though hurricanes give it the semblance of more, a more organic, let us say, activity. They walk along the breakwater by the beach. Is it Mother slipped on the rocks, and broke her arm? Or Aunt Bernice? One did. The visit of the friend, the woman — they report it as most pleasant. They are impressed, perhaps even displaced by intimidation, that she is so obviously socially *well-fixed* — they smell it with old habits. My aunt. My mother. Aunt Bernice tells story of her first employment, in a one room factory, in a sort of warehouse, where they are put to work, she and the other girls, affixing hat bands to hats, and since they are apprentices, receive nothing for this work, but are told that in a few weeks they will be sufficiently competent to be paid, like the other girls they are told are behind the door, in another room adjacent, who are being paid. Then one day, the employer absent, they get sufficient nerve to open the door, and see the girls on the other side, who, like themselves, have been told the same story. So they all protest. And quit. How one thinks — how true, there is only *one* condition.

BAR TALK. Bartok, just the same thing, in this case, like the piano scenes he'd write for children, kids, you might say, play like the bear walks through that forest, and woof, woof, not like that, but of course the drunken bear dances in crazy cadenzas, and in the bar the light falls, goes, the length of that long wooden surface. You could scream at them, hey, let's play Bartok — one of those middle Europeans had joy in his heart.

All serious people end up being serious. All whites white, all blacks black — so they say. Intellectuals are people got sex in the head, would Lawrence say, because they can't get it up, or once up, down. There was a story, told years ago, and last night repeated, about Orwell, was in bar with working people, ordered drink for working man next him, a pint, which is supposed to be read as question, no says he, have to get out of here soon, a half pint will do; says Orwell, but that's not what people of your class want, it's a pint, or nothing. It really is nothing. The syntax all dislocated. No working man would be that patient, to hear the end.

It must be the person does, even unintentionally, precede the definition. Now pay attention to your class, which must be Aristotle again. Play with your own kind. But they won't talk to me, much less indulge in games with me. Never you mind, those are your people. But they got a funny look to them. Never mind, them's it for you, young man. Oh, is that what I am — or is? Or what is that, on you. I's your ma — well, not like that, I'm your mother, whence, from which, and to for, your eyes are decently averted. Not look at your own mother, but instead at them dirty things? Keep to your kind, lad — not do, to mix.

Buddy's comment upon Max, who had told Julie, *yellowbird*, he called her that too once, when the revolution comes, or he must have had use of another vocabulary, not such a dull one, like wind the clock, it's the end of the week, pay day sort of stuff, no revolution there — oh dear, the wheel's going round — no, he said, when the revolution comes, you've got to go, all your sort, blonde aryans, or whatever term he used to describe of course the very delightful blue-eyed blonde-haired softness of her person, no less her heart, dear, very sweet girl she was always, in all the confusions she did experience with men, source of all evil, they only want one thing, but circumstances, which needed her, first time met in fog, that haze of L.A., stopped for a moment at the intersection, turning on, the roach passing round, look out to see the car adjacent, shades, glasses, also shades, also turning on, with the white headed white gloved possibly policeman in the middle of said intersection, get the hell out of there, that's revolution, later, had she come home then, or been there all the the time, like out in field, somehow a town, of oil derricks, a house, someone, the wife was it, is passing a plate of pot, and some opium, smoke, and the master of the house, an incredible and serious young man, person, plays baritone, onk, onk, and crazy guttural under-ride of sounds he should live in the cellar, but at least no neighbors, drive home, their home, Julie's, through L.A., to drive two Porsches back to Albuquerque, Race, and Buddy, and him. This was yellowbird — instant love therefor, and also her sweet shrewd husband Manny, a local boy, played trumpet, later in crazy dinge of N.Y. was waiter sat in, you dig, on relaxed occasions, with the band.

All that. No, comes the revolution, baby, you got to go — despite subsequent hook, of junk, another husband, bull fighter, at least on the way, all the way she went, each time, with must have been physical condition just as much as the toothache she has first meeting, all her lovely mouth swollen, so sweet, like a bee stung. Like bartoc, bar none — Max, you play it. Tell how make her the one meets the edge, no color, but her the so-called victim. Would rather kick a dead horse, i.e., he'd understand. She comes back, tells Buddy, in perplexity, but Max says, comes the revel, which is the misspelling, the revolution, I have to go. Like, your mother's calling. All into damnwell fade, now. Max freaked on speed, or not to propose like libel, like, he was never the one.

EXPERIENCE (in a manner usual enough) created by a system —
The spatial relations made by a house, for example, the distri-
bution of movement in an arrangement of streets, etc. Ralph
Ellison's use of the term, *conscious consciousness* — apropos his
proposal of Malraux's *Man's Fate* as an instance of a 'classic'
text — mind experience, or however to isolate it if that's possible, taken as the possibility of system.

Watching the markedly tall man leaving the dining room — he
makes the actually over-large hallway and stairs going up to the
lobby seem of a size his own body is the measure of, i.e., it's his
size, not the overly big space others make of it. Now there is an
awkwardness in the size of this typewriter, the way the keys are
placed almost 'beside it' — in front — so that its literal opera-
tion seems to be somehow in another place, as one types. The
resistant difficulty it seems to make of the action of thinking, in
words, that this form of writing seems to be —

The days' form, the wondering rather insistently just what one
is 'doing' here, and yet much liking, also, the kind of intensities
the literally random talking of the afternoons, with the so-called
students — actually a pleasantly dense and various collection of
young and happily fresh-feeling younger human beings. Letting
it be there, much like 'letting the song lie in itself.' Paying attention — letting the fact of the circumstance come out. So bor-
ing does seem the alternative, among many others, god knows,
of trying to give it 'point ,' to direct it to some 'purpose .' What is
that purpose, unless clearly one of a very immediate and direct
context of, the building's on fire, that door will get you out —
or else, to share in the doing of this, and/or to do it yourself, like
they say, these skills and materials are needed. At some point,
perhaps invariably, the relation between this thing being done,

or being used in the doing of something possibly else, and the information system used to convey the fact or nature of its occasion to another — The occasion of so-called abstraction *there*, in fact, the experience then of that "there," as opposed — really — to *here* — I. A. Richards speaking of his method of teaching people who've had great difficulty in learning to read and write, his use of the *tensions* in language systems, — not that, this, here, there, now, and so on.

Whether errors, as meaning to write *Echoes* becomes *Whether*, as the finger meant to strike the E key, hits the W — and the thought moves to include it, to use it in the thought, and so on.

Echoes. And, ands. Possible possibilities.... Syntax making articulate, i.e., coming literally to sound in the context, fact of fatigue and distraction. The machine talking too, as one fumbles in use of it. Barking doors. Crying tables. Spilt lights. All that clutter — book at that moment falling down back of typewriter, so that head becomes attentive and yields momently to record of it, and now is again back in the difficulty of the typewriter, how wide the paper is, where is one, or where are the words now in their occupation of the paper — how much left, to go, to be said before the end of it has been come to. How much time is there left. The ease of it, also — being tired, wants to relax in that continuum, to yawn, stretch, let go of attention as a preoccupation. What's that all about.

Bill wants a situation, call it, wherein he can take a daily photo of himself — he was talking with Marisol — that can accumulate that content of a face, nothing fancy, just getting up, a sort of business like the slot-machine photo booths, like you wash your face, take a picture, go about the day's content as ever. So that you get a year's accumulation of face, so recorded. Like Bob, yesterday, involved with a photograph that tracks movement, in the essentially static context of the photo-image itself — so that you 'anchor' the image by having some of its detail, anything, or one, or more, stay in very particularized containment of focus, very sharp; and then let the hand, head, whatever, move — and with strobes, you get a one, two, three phasing manifest in the image. Like Bobbie's 'trace' in the move of objects on Xerox. Like this — writing — "fitful tracing . . . . " No copies, nor intent, nor much at all — but *phases*, be they phases of the moon. Or mine(d). Or the *d* added, and paper gone.

WHATEVER IT WAS they must have been thinking about, they were there too, certainly, as much as the rest, like they say. Funny what they hear, or seem to. 'Objective, for example, becomes a sense of something apart from oneself, something in the world — though what 'world' or how 'in,' it must be they can't then think of. Age again, possibly — being young. Always that insistent organism 'doing its own thing' — being one. Fascinated by modes of age, really, especially in girls somehow — is it the fact of sexual complement, being male, one is drawn to, or just that it is a denser, more various condition. Possibly.

At the curiously dense house of people visited on Sunday, a very pleasant, large and comfortable house, very socially comfortable — at first surrounded by the young, so that the hostess, a straight-seeming vigorous woman in her forties, attractive, suggests the study would be a quieter, more relaxed place for all thus interested to be. There, literally, one sits with them all surrounding, all young, with one exception of the older woman has

some specific question in mind to ask, something literary —
whereas they either look at one intensely, measuring, or else try
it on, their own condition, especially the young women. Of which
there is one unequivocal beauty, tall, very relaxed sense of flesh,
black hair, looking always a little flushed, pleasantly so, a little
arrogant in manner, sharp, quick eyes, pouting, like a 19th century heroine. Wears very large, round, charming glasses. A
young woman of no little means, one would think.

Lovely, as it were, to be the village blacksmith, at least doing
something can be attended, taken as literal and having an active information. Remembering Tom, when still very young, in
Mallorca, caught in the chaos and, to him, it must have been,
terror of the occasion, a pig-killing, goes directly to the man he
feels most securely — who is, in fact, the man killing the pig,
hence the center of all that energy.

Where do they come from, where do they go — etc. Lovely the
round and around of it, over and over and over. Delicious people
— as the man, yesterday, in the coffee shop one's come to, for a
coke, so dry in the goddamn mouth at that point, as it's time to
go, notes the tape recorder, he's apparently the owner of the
place, and asks what it is. Then, as he is told, shows in turn a
watch he has on his wrist, which needs no winding, runs by
means of an electronically stimulated 'vibration' — and says,
listen to it. So that one puts it to the ear and hears a sharp,
insistent, rather high-pitched humming. Like some incredible
seashell.

Lovely all — days, the tiredness accumulating and time become
phase of immediate temper and energy. Crazy wash and fall of
water remembered as a kid, living then in Northeast Harbor,

Maine — that endlessly insistent movement. Could never make any meaning of it. Whitman most to be respected in his sense of it, "Out of the cradle endlessly rocking . . . ." Not, god knows, the metaphor only, but the "cradle, endlessly, rocking . . . ." The words themselves that don't stop.

Would track along, down, otherwise, brooks — most in spring, would follow, thinking to come to some place they led to. Had somehow the conviction, though more felt then as simple feeling, 'they led some place.' Very intrigued by sense you could go from town to town, following brooks, which in turn became rivers, which in turn at last gained the sea. One winter, things so froze you could skate from West Acton to South Acton, on Teel's Brook, and did so, having to jump over branches and roots, and hummocks, had frozen at points in the ice, oneself and a friend, or possibly more, all the way, till at last it widens and you come to the pond that sits, or then did, under the railroad bridge, must have been a small factory there somewhere, and made a great space of ice. Back a year ago, very strange seeing that brook, could have been stepped over, with a slight hop, filled for the most part with a wavy marsh grass and cat tails, and occasional skunk cabbages too. All shrunk as somehow one hadn't really thought would be the case, though many indeed attest to it. Imagining life as growing, growing — into a giant, a huge illimitable form.

VOICE FROM LOVELY NOWHERE — Art Murphy, young guy had set some poems, also worked with Williams' material, was at that time at Juilliard, friend of Paul Zukofsky's — was struck by what he'd taken to use, also the translation, into sound, really a spatial situation, of what the words were as material. Someone later saying it's like Webern? Perhaps — but how else does one come into it. It always sounds like something else, at first, then makes itself or else stops.

The dumdedumdum, dumdum, accents — can hear the prose sound same, up above there, "Voice from lovely nowhere . . . . " Always from lovely nowhere.

That girl saying, lovely exact face, quite long, that well-washed long blonde hair young ladies of good families do seem to favor, saying, she'd been at the Country Day School for ten years, over half her actual life, at this point. That was the family sense of the place, as the other woman said, we have the younger children come to these events, because we feel they are taught effectually by the experience of the older ones, and so on, and so. Or again, of the young lady — her teeth in bands, made her at times close her mouth, as one shared the seat, back, with her on the ride returning to the hotel, awkward a bit because of them — horrid things to put on teeth, in one's mouth, most awkward sans any question. Such a pleasant long straight nose, high forehead, good clear grey blue sort of eyes. All of them look usefully healthy, good breeders one thinks — not at all uglily.

But like Karen's crazy mut female dog, wispy, terrier, bristly hair, incredible energy of excitement, endless restlessness, provoked by any movement in a wild range of feelings — *that* has survived, leaped through, come without that breeding, just *made it*. Always moved god knows by that occasion, just the *luck* of it.

So back to Art, who's there in that same school now, for the same arts festival business, with Steve Reich, who is thus by the young people's bulletin identified: "STEVE REICH has been composer/

performer at the San Francisco tape and music center, at Yale University and at the New School . . . . " Und so weiter.

Time really now insistent, e.g., in one hour, for example. Will that then be there forever? Where, etc. In one hour. In one hour there are sixty minutes, or then the division into seconds, but has to be place to be in one, or any, for that matter. I.e., when it's not in one hour, it will be in another.

Thought you'd like to hear so having a minute, would just drop a line. To say, thought you'd like to hear, so having a minute. So have a minute, thought, to hear. You'd like to. All that sort of stuff you never put anywhere anyhow, it just comes in, goes out, up and down, in and out the system, as Buckminster Fuller says — one thinks one heard that — Or music: Go in and out the system, go in and out the system, go in and out the system — Words then misplaced, forgotten, i.e., how it ends there. Something about roses, it seemed it was. Not a mulberry bush in any case.

He looked through them all and found no cases of mulberry etc. Case dismissed. Next case. That's television. But pleasant to think, would you please rerun that. Like, who's rerunning this business. Who's recharged here.

Such a card. Not comic however — nor intent to be. At all. Not at all funny. Ferlinghetti: if I told them my mother just died, they'd break up. The rest of the story is really another story. Well, his, among others, also hers, obviously, if she's implied as dying. Them too, since they're the ones got it started in the first place. If they hadn't laughed all evening, at anything he'd said, he wouldn't have said that. That wouldn't have been anything then to say, but something else. He said enough, surely, to make his point. At least it was understood, what he was saying, even if what he otherwise said was not. That's what it was all about.

SOMETHING THAT STICKS in mind, actually a familiar question — why are the arts insistent on technological possibility. But more, does writing involve that same interest — etc., etc. Etc. Of course. Etc. Phasing. System again, really — or wanting some information as to the context, call it, in which language is being experienced. Not simply to be told, like they say, to go to bed or whatever, but to have use of how one is hearing that, literally. Not 'psychologically' — but as physical situation. Always fascinated by Olson's move/ment — a literal situation of phasing, manifest in the words. Or Duncan, almost like tape loops — in fact, very much like them, not at all 'metaphorically'. One of the people in the so-called class remarking Beethoven's means of working, not 'linearly' as, now this is done, now done, now that is to be done, now that — but in a situation almost spatial (he was speaking of the drafts of the 5th symphony, of B/s taking this from that, and putting it in there, then taking that out, putting in something else, so that the material was both an accumulation and a collection variably possible, i.e., could be 'shifted around' in a various formal situation, etc. Too, John Linsley's interest to explore neural and physiological relations in language, to possibly make explicit Olson's proposals about breath and speech relations, and also the 'proprioceptive' — again much insistent on the contextual, as agency.

— Spill of names now, losing ability to identify who it is has been met, and now reappears. E.g., have apparently made arrangements to talk to a man, at noon, and find that it was actually two men, but go off with the first, leaving the second to arrive and find no one there — but happily no hurt feelings, like they say, but again, what can be the sense this man has, having made what seems to him an agreeably simple arrangement to meet for conversation, and he finds he's been mistaken for another man — who in turn is unaware of any of it. Must be some sense of his faintness, inability to make himself known to others — while the case is simply too many faces, voices, people, too much to thus locate and remember, as Allen once confronted by young man in someplace like San Francisco, who says, remember me?, can only answer, if your life did not actually involve mine in some intensive manner, some event of relation would make a focus for memory, I am afraid I really can't. And yet one obviously does want to be remembered, especially by someone, as Allen, one very much admires and wants a place with. So he'd take them all, if he could, but it's just not possible. Bound to get lost in it, something inevitably left behind.

— One's own so-called identity becomes equally vague, so much is separated from how it is one would feel, or possibly act, with another company. Fact of sudden direct intimacies, call them, pushed on people in the most social of gatherings, just that that habit (at home) is so much the so-called case of one's way of being with others it 'will out etc.

The lady speaking at dinner of, was it your father's book (this, to another younger woman there) that described his wife's intention not to have the children be fearful of their bodies by themselves going about naked in the house. The other answers, I was the only child, perhaps my uncle? No, it was your father's book — and then another woman speaks of their intent, hers and her husband's, to do the same thing — and found their oldest daughter was extremely fearful, in school, of being nude in front of the other children, for showers, examinations, etc. All of that curiously awkward and false psychology, i.e., that proposes *a* must be followed by *b* — but so often misplaces what might be called the 'terms.' I didn't know it was loaded. No, he didn't even know it was a 'gun' —

But now. But "tired," still — what does that propose to describe? A so-called level of energy, possibly, a way of feeling the body respond, as going up and down stairs, shade of some sense possibly a cold is being contracted? For? Cigarettes very harsh — no 'desire' in the sense, really no sexual response to anything. The real comfort, moments before sleep, then also, just at waking. A grey-like warmth.

Home now — a deep relaxation, of feeling, also a restlessness permeates much response, to others here, Sarah, Kate, or Bobbie. But the *physical* relief, the letting go — fucking, or eating, talking, moving about the house now in one's own body, a great need happily resolved.

Ron called last night to tell me of John's sudden, absolutely unexpected death. They had been together, with Billy Al Bengston, etc., at a party — later, as Billy Al and John left, apparently not long after John had heart attack, dead shortly after if not then and there. Described as a "massive coronary." A very few years older than myself, perhaps one or two, but no more. Bobbie's saying, this will happen more frequently now, as a gauge obviously of what will be increasingly our own experience. As Frank O'Hara's death then. But neither does she mean, nor would I, some curious 'economy' of that possibility. Somehow I knew one would die when about eighteen, i.e., physically experienced that limit, and then came upon it again aged about thirty-five.

I couldn't feel a regret for John's death — he *was* dead, when I heard, instantly had become that somehow. What I felt myself relieved by was so close to that sense, of Allen's, "Death's let you out . . . " but not in sense of 'escape' but that it had occurred as an instant, merciful, in human sense, no long painful lingering of the knowledge of limit and impending death. I couldn't make that, couldn't at all, for a friend. Fear at times my mother, aunt, will be momently in that bitter economy. I *know* people die. Then let it be *quick*.

Elsewise — a swirl somehow to things, to relationships. I sense the friends we do have here, really the one couple we might be utterly open with — not that others god knows don't prove friends also, but it is really that intuitive economy, that knowledge, of others I am speaking of — that things are hard for them, she's off to a job she much wants, needs, and will be respected by, as a visiting potter, he restless in himself, wanting reassurance therefor from another 'age', younger, or whatever, wants the casual perhaps. She is impatient with that, I sense. A funny, fucking world at times. So many — is it again some fact of 'biological' age? Or doddering fools. Or what the hell. I seem intent on making everything the condition, dependent, on everything else. Lovely note in Tom's letter: "I have just finished writing a paper for theo. on what truth was. I said it was relative naturally . . . ." He's had a history teacher he spoke of when visiting last month, who apparently had told him *all* condition of person could be described, and/or was determined, by terms of social, physical environment. That's ass-end-to, one wanted to say — just that it isn't known, or *what* isn't known, 'until later' (like what you may get for Xmas etc.), is *not* experienced in hindsight (or is only thus regarded) only. Even that banal story of the 'little locomotive', *I think I can, I think I can,* is preferable to that teacher's dreary and perhaps called for stoicism.

At last. Jim Dine writes: "i just returned from a football match, and i am frozen and bruised. my oldest son and i were thrown and crunched to the ground by a partisan crowd. these english are a queer bunch . . . . " Allen, also recent card: " "Leaky lifeboat" Gregory C. said about the body — it certainly doesn't stand up to the cosmic metal crunch — so maybe I'm all wrong about wanting to "feel" "good." Help! down the drain again! Gotta get new Metaphysics! . . . "

NAGGING SENSE of not having got to it yet, i.e., best done with in whatever manner it can be, before I fall off completely, at something like four in the afternoon. But had woke up so early, or equally from the other end, late, hardly able to keep eyes open etc. Not that bad really — just dazed, as driving down to the postoffice again, had hazy senses, at moments, the car was drifting, which it probably was. One thing interesting: stepping out to get to the car, i.e., out the door, had sudden sharp dusty smell, like the smell of a day, had not smelled quite like that for some time, years, in fact. It may be that smoking cigars only is proving its point, whatever it is, at least beyond impossibly burned mouth it seems from eight in the morning till whatever hour one goes to sleep.

Gabbling, really. Note all of this, i.e., e.g., etc., all seem to start with, I guess they are, noun clusters, what did they call them — substantive clauses. The one thing Santa isn't. Faint humor indeed makes the day even greyer, although the sun shines almost fiercely, despite so-called winter, and the blue of sky is almost metallically clear etc.

Bobbie and the girls coming in now, can hear them at other end of us (had meant to say "house") — Kate saying, "mommy," etc. Funny how they enter on a lean of some purpose, want, etc. Elsewise they are silent, and say nothing. She's also in now. Can hear her too, talking back. Sort of a scutter of sounds back there, makes a kind of pitch of babble against the tv, other end though closer, hence heard more distinctly, but also rejected, hence not.

Why woke so early, was sense, in dream, person I'd depended on to take and play tapes for classes, hadn't, so I then had to face either enraged (I doubt they would ever be so, for such reason — too sluggish about such expectations) or contemptuous students. That's a dream — faint sneering faces, "But I tried to help you!" Oneself pleading, "It was all I knew how to say!" Aie . . . Must be sense from previous years of teaching when at times the relation, with the Students, was almost of necessity a politic solicitude. Their parents the custodians, no, the owners, of possibility. They hired one etc. Or the so-called headmaster did, but was their servant also. The fact of what does happen persistently to teachers, all forms of it, no matter 'high' or 'low'. Remember at U.B.C. that summer, Allen meeting the visiting professors from Toronto, talking, then asking one, what he was doing — and the answer, "I'm only a teacher . . . . " Rank with self-contempt, so much so it sounds only faintly. His own imagination of its being the lowest of the low. So — what *does* that have to do with "Oh fathers and teachers . . . . " Another order of reality altogether. I can't imagine teaching from a feeling of self-contempt or even a sense one was worthless etc. Have obviously come close, in several very specific situations — as, for one, teaching in Guatemala where Joe would tell me, "The reason I pay that man more to run the *finca* store, is because he is worth more, it's more important etc." So that was that, or whatever it was — god knows. Joe must have driven himself finally too fast, into a box of some kind, he had a crazily persistent wish to kill himself — but almost gaily, it seemed, no real sadness in it, just an absolutely clear sense of 'ending it' that way. What was sad was his love for his wife, who couldn't, it so appeared at least, really 'credit' him with that feeling, or wouldn't, more accurately, accept it. She really didn't like him much. But I did, and so did Bobbie I think — there was a very human toughness, and perception, and gentleness to him. But I don't know finally, in that he was 'my boss' — an odd use of that possessive pronoun, as Bob B . . . once said. All said one way or another — I can't really believe it's more than a 'thing to be doing', and that's what it's all about. I. e., talking.

FADING OFF — mind rising, at best, much like fish used to, in bottom of pool, coming up slowly in a series of spiraling circles. When was that. West Acton, again. Somewhere back there — as though time were a distance, and it is most often, it seems, imagined as such, the fading wake, etc.

A brief catalog of plans, like they say: summer to be spent in the house in Annisquam, where we'd been two summers ago. Get out of this one — possibly sell it? Come June. Not much else in mind — no more thought of now to do, than what I sit here literally writing. So-called books about to be: *Pieces, A Quick Graph, The Charm*. Even to name such possibilities used to be like telling beads. Now, not so much.

What is that useful sense of the 'future' — viz, its occurrence resolves all conjecture. Words to that effect, i.e., on hands and knees trying to find book (P. W. Bridgeman's writing apropos, specifically the discussion of *time*), am confused by sense of where it should be, in the muddle of the bookshelves back of me, and then remember, or do I, Moe has it — something he wanted to read for himself there, respectably enough. But why not then get the damn thing back. Ah well again. *If* he has it to begin with. So it goes on, actually another 'track' from what the 'real' might be supposed to consist of — but which is so-called which, and where is it one is, in either. Or elsewhere. I get now altered sense of, "But that was in another country. And besides, the wench is dead. . . ." Like Olson's report from Whorf of Hopi sense: what's happening over *there* cannot be accepted as happening at the same time as what's happening *here*. Space is a time modifier. Try catching a train that ain't there.

Through the wall, hear in a curious intimacy — in the pleasant almost cubicle of the workroom I have, Donovan's singing, Sarah playing it. She's probably in the kitchen, or in Asia — having seen to that. But no, sudden lift of her own voice, singing just over his, through the wall. Now she must be putting another record on, hear her moving it, and what's she's done is to replay the one just heard. I love that sense, though obviously its real occasion might be hopeless indeed, of making scratching noises, or banging, to be heard through walls, rock, that "I hear them!" Awful when the fact of men caught in a collapsed mine shaft. Awful, as kid, that one must have been somewhere in Pennsylvania, days it lasted, crazy scratching kind of possibility. *"I hear them!"* Somehow hope contained still in the utterly hopeless fact of something. Time passes.

The man met briefly in Lake Forest, at the Deerpath Inn, we were all having lunch, speaking of Poe's house in Baltimore I think. How it was in poor repair, should be some sort of state concern or whatever to keep it in repair — but what he then described as Poe's bedroom, and how one got to it, a very actual garret not permitting one to stand, not him at least, reached by a stair so low and so constricted he was on his hands and knees in order to squeeze through, into it. And Poe's young wife then on the floor below, to which the stairs led apparently, and the woman attached (aunt?) in bedroom adjacent not even separated from the wife's room, but more in the order of a sitting room adjoining. All there: the claustrophobic sense of enclosure, the paranoia about being surprised in some act.

Imagination of one's own life. Boat still? A thing taken in hand, found there — what one could do with oneself, all the sexual echo, or implication, of that. No wonder the head and heart got separated — one had to be left outside. Anyhow — not for long, at all, at all. Or goes on thinking, in the night, hours after, *working* — which has root somewhere back there in to 'make sacrifice'. It's the same.

"To tell what subsequently I saw, and what heard . . . . " Williams — also like Allen's "What did I notice? Particulars!" Brought again and again to fact of, what is it — here, there. The time of it. Agency's modality, i.e., my own.

Conversation: what will you have for lunch, Alan. We don't eat lunch, Alan . . . . Unexpected visit now, he'd come flying in apparently last night around five, from NYC — there with John, I guess. Anyhow a simple man to get on with, and with an interesting condition, like they say — the habits, orders, of a wealthy Englishman — Irishman, more literally, as he would remind one, etc. Having just put his rented car, a Mustang, on edge of bank backend of house (here), so it's all about to slide down same, happily now moves it sans problem — and is off to park it elsewhere. Contrast I keep thinking of, that is, his intent of a couple of years ago, to make movie in Yucatan centered on Maya — and ends up with John making *The Secret Life of Hernando Cortez* starring Taylor Mead and Ultra Violet. Like, some resolution of that hope. Have not seen film — though think I'm old enough — which is, apparently, interminably fucking in variety of situations, places, etc. Talking to John at Xmas, he says: objectifying, reifying, all that range of sexual fact — so as to 'place' it, so as to see it as there, etc. Something like that. Céline, early in novel (*Castle to Castle*), makes point: words make limp dicks, or words make soft pricks, or (better) words make pricks soft. Cock softer. Mullen-sucker. Bong-banger. Ideas are not always appropriate, no more than the sun shines forever where the sun is always shining. Thinking: that bit of Zukofsky's, "a dog that runs never lies down . . . . " "A dog, *that* runs, never lies down . . . . " He says. I was thinking: *that* runs, and the dog keeps on lying down? And did you get the license plate number sir etc. How about a sir etcetera and a glass of mud. Two over lightly, and fork.

Anyhow *that* Alan is here, the other Alan — there are many Alans in the world at one time, but only one by one do they seem evident — or ask the question: will all those named Alan please signify by raising their right hand. No one does, i.e., no one here other than Bob, Robert, Bobby, boy man — Boyman. Willie Boyman. You put your little foot right here, and your left foot right here, and your right foot right here, and there. Burble through walls again. The one so-called constant. The other Alan saying, in NYC a winter ago — the psychic energy of so many people in the buildings surrounding, can literally feel the weight of its force, pushing on him etc. Squeezing his head possibly into shape of insufficient turnip. A lone blade of grass on a broken sandhill. Echoes. The pun they couldn't kill. Eccos. Necco wafers. Thinking of 'future' — somewhere in time and space there awaits some number like fifteen people, various sorts and sizes, expect to be dealt with in some manner for period of two hours — in roughly two hours.

Gap then of some fifteen, twenty minutes — no evidence of same immediately clear, to me at least. So could write one word, say, wait ten minutes, twenty, hour, hours, day, days, weeks, months, years, — but there the limit does begin to be manifest, like they say — and so on. No one the wiser. And what would be 'hidden' — in some intent — to begin with? Ho, ho. You thought I just wrote it straight out, like. But I didn't. I wrote one word. Waited five days. But think of the arithmetic and/or is it *possible*, mind you, is it possible to write (how much?) in what length of time, given that means of proceeding. Can we *wait* for it. Would you rather sit in the car. Are you tired, of waiting. What, are you waiting for. Why wait. A simple downpayment secures your order.

THE MESCALIN CLEARED out a lot of gunk, just that tensions and an almost active depression apropos the time now to be got through before we can leave had become increasingly difficult to deal with. We went — Bobbie and I — first to meet Bill

Merwin and company for dinner. No one showed for about a half hour, which was pleasant enough, i.e., Bobbie had spent most of the afternoon getting through a birthday party for Kate (which also went happily), and I went over to their school, to talk to kids interested in writing, etc. So the time in the restaurant, waiting for the others, was a useful chance to unwind. Then, after the reading — the kids now at their grandmother's for the weekend — we went to a party back in Placitas, then came back to our house about twelve or so, and decided to take the mescalin.

I wasn't sure just how much would be needed, but wanted to avoid the awful dragging waiting of the previous business of the acid given us about a month before — which must have been mostly 'speed' and left me particularly with a frustrated sense of nothing ever really taking off. Like waiting in the bus station, for the damn bus that never gets there. Anyhow this time, wisely or not, I took what we had, some six pills of one batch, and two of another, and split them, and we took them all. Wisely enough — since any less would have been another drag, and as it was, we had mainly four to six hours of useful float, mainly verbal — in fact, without visual shifts of any marked order at all — and a great sense of a cleaning out of tensions, and then a very happy sense of inner peace and relaxation. Too, I loved the intensity of verbal play — even to lovely physical experience of words' sound in my head and mouth. Very happy clarity. Later, — it must have been nine or ten in the morning — Bobbie went then to sleep, and I spent about four hours sitting in the livingroom listening to records and reading — Sappho, for one, which book I must have had for almost a year without really reading it. Then Beckett's poems, as:

what would I do without this world faceless incurious
where to be lasts but an instant where every instant
spills in the void the ignorance of having been
without this wave where in the end
body and shadow together are engulfed . . .

What becomes — to my own mind deeply useful — so explicit
with either mescalin, or acid, is the *finite* system of the *form* of
human-body life, i.e., that that phase, call it, of energy qua form
is of no permanent order whatsoever, in the single instance, however much the species' form is continued genetically, etc. That
night, with the mescalin, I had insistently in my head this earlier
poem of my own, called "The Skeleton":

The element in which they live,
the shell going outward until
it never can end, formless,
seen on a clear night as stars,
the term of life given them
to come back to, down to,
and then to be in
themselves only, only skin.

Which had then the edge of obvious irony, previous to that information I've been talking about — but now is altogether the
obvious, and yet sans edge of fear any longer, or even so-called
regret. That the 'I' can accept its impermanent form and yet realize the energy-field, call it, in which it is one of many, also *one*.
Nothing, in that sense, as Louis says, can ever leave.

ALL THE PLEASURE of the last two days somehow lost as tedium recurs, the week starts again — though the weather is good, in fact, dazzling, sharp blue sky, springlike. The house somehow on us, on me — and I land it on Bobbie — as *thing* now makes an impossibly heavy limit as to what can be next. Sits as dead center for endless self-depression. I feel disloyal to it, having had such pleasure in it, earlier. Must be literal *fact* of so-called objects is unacceptable. That nothing can be held on to, and that which holds on in reverse — as this house is now somehow our 'responsibility' — is deadlier than attachments the other way round. Like children who never leave home.

But more to the point — I hate leaving. I hate what was the hope of something proving thus limit and dilemma. I hate the damn baggage one gets willynilly attached to, and then has to push off, each time a little more restlessly, yet with less energy in that act. I feel a deadly tiredness, and what prove 'solutions' and/or small victories of so-called intention are inevitably the same dreary accumulation and drabness. There's nothing comes of it. Children don't grow to succeed their parents' ambitions. Nothing has that pattern in any sense one can respect. This morning, driving back here from the city, I picked up two kids, like tattered gypsies, seeming about 16 or so — 'on the road' and headed for the hippy community just above us, The Lower Farm. Despite the fadedness, already, of both of them, the kind of vague, passive excitement — the 'lore' of their situation, and the half-furtive manner they at times use as address — at least they are in the world unequivocally, I mean they are literally on the road, in a fact of their own bodies, literally somewhere. No imagination of them ever quite gets them there elsewise — certainly not that of their parents with mom's tears and dad's irritation. Fuck 'em all . . . .

Were one to change, so to speak — the impulse would be so located, just to drop the whole fucking mess of such context. Let damn well go of it. Is life, so to speak, like the village idiot who's given a job polishing the town's cannon, in the square, and then saves all the money given him — finally gives up the job, and when asked why, says, he's now bought his own cannon. Would that be the best of its apparent occasion — "self-action," as Olson would say. Seeing this morning, in a letter, title of an earlier book of Tom Raworth's — *The Relation Ship* — but what about Lawrence's death ship, "The Ship of Death": "The apples falling like great drops of dew/ to bruise themselves an exit from themselves . . . . " Something of that onus in the house, itself now some curious scab of previous condition, to be shed like that, picked off and got rid of — no longer a place made clear in living, at all.

Cage's sense again, that motels suffice as 'homes' — that all the locatable shell of usual existence has to break down, and be let go of — all that impinges so insistently as purpose, gain, success in intention. Fearful, one realizes the house as shared vocabulary — that each time one's let go of, all its accumulated resonance falls too. What then to move to, but the place of whatever renewal of energies seems to be possible? Isn't that why, in this point of age, there is fear of losing relationship, being 'dropped,' just that the place one can make for another diminishes as energies also do — or seem to, except as frustration provokes them — sad, sad echo of Dennie's poem: "We have not spoken of these tired/ risings of the sun . . . . " Or the fantasies, my own so often, of Bobbie's shift off from me sexually, to someone else — not as it used to be, in my head, almost a warcry of belligerent suspicion, i.e., a rush of anger and dismay — but now, half-curious, in my mind, a sense of provision, a sly shift, an acknowledgment of my own change of condition. An accommodation without alternatives.

INSISTENT BREAKUP of forms, things. Sister calling this noon, or a little after, mother had called her from Florida, unlikely it now seems that Aunt Bernice will survive. Eighty-five she is, having still insistently told the doctor (even now) she's seventy-six. The women draw together I sense — though Helen says mother had mislaid, understandably, my telephone number (which I'd sent her again only a few days previous). So Helen will go, must now be enroute there — and I'm to call on Friday, when it will be noon there, to see how things are. My mother apparently much upset now, crying on the phone, Helen said — she'd been, previously, such an adamant containment of her emotions, must have been trained to that both by having been a nurse, and also, when my father died, the necessity of carrying on, not showing what must have been her actual situation. Not necessarily a poverty thereby enforced — but bleak, surely, at times, not to let go, let it wash out, in an openness of other people, her literal family.

She's old now too. Can't be much less than Aunt Bernice, and Helen says, on the phone, she must now think of herself as next — that damn history again, the chronological — though it so rarely proves the actual sequence, as my own father's death would demonstrate, or John Altoon's — or so many, from the war, or otherwise. The chance, that changes all of it. There's no listing proves the way it has to be as 1,2,3, etc.

I don't know. I don't feel grief as yet. Helen says she is not conscious, recognizes no one apparently. I like her, love her, almost shyly. No real occasion, like they say, we should have such feeling for one another — but what I sensed in her, I think, even as a boy, was that she really liked men — was that incorrigible though proper coquette. Delighted doctors, among others — "your sister is quite a lady . . . . " That kind of report our mother would then tell us of, later. The care she took with herself, in that sense — despite the awkwardness of the colostomy, for her of all people — her, not daintiness, but very literal feminity. Her impatience, with either self-indulgent sentiment or any attempt to get round some actual state of feeling. Sneer, she would — very truly. Tough — yet respectful, somehow, of actual innocence in men, that tender state — as my Uncle Ward, despite the impatience she often seemed to feel with him, his unwitting sillinesses, and his dogged loyalty to his previous and very much dead first wife — he had named their daughter Thoreau — which drove her up the wall with irritable impatience. But never, I felt, simply she wanted someone to lean on — wanted really, always, more than that, a context, one might say — a man. Was discreet, but had to have one, unlike my mother somehow — who made other adjustments, having children, ourselves. And density of persons, at first at least, the job — with all the various patients — then the household, with Theresa (the girl effectually rescued from home for the feeble-minded by my father, who comes to work for us, then, after his death, stays on, and is really the closest and most stable person I have to relate to, as a daily event in the house, all the years I'm growing up). Then grandmother, grandfather — both lovely, tough people — my aunt much their complex, grandfather's will and emotion, grandmother's will and wit (which, though seemingly cold, I can remember as a very actual smile, to herself often, of what charms both awkwardness and its concomitant humanness do combine). A deeply decent, straight woman — makes both my mother and aunt, and the humanity of my Uncle Will — who was the happy nature somehow, of that family, as my uncle, younger, Uncle Hap(py), was very decisively not. His the will elsewise: five years our next-door neighbor, with his sullen family, decides on impulse and 'reason' not to speak to me, myself aged about 14 forward. Aunt Bernice never accepted that shit, bless her. She knew.

BACK HERE YESTERDAY, about three or so — come from Salt Lake, first east across the mountains to Denver, then down, so that we come in over Taos, then down following the mountains to Albuquerque. A deep wash of nostalgia. Upland meadows, bowls, filled now with snow. A scale that much attracts me, a dry asperity to things, distances — a great range of space, horizontally balanced.

Then, having drunk some on plane, at home continue, in somewhat desultory manner, and turn on when Bobbie's gone to the store — a float then, which lasts much of the evening, going on, with brief time at Bill P/s house, having gone down, Bobbie and me, with Steve Katonah and friends. Sitting all in front of big tv set, like a fire — two lovely kids, girls, about six and three — hierarchal look to each, the older, sharp, very tense quick look, likes being placed in mind games, e.g., that everything in my house is named "Creeley." The younger, blonde with classic short braids, great apple cheeks, very alert kid — and finally both come up close to where I'm sitting on the floor, make themselves beds of blankets and sleeping bags, curl up by my legs, and I can then reach over to tuck them in. Sharp insistent nostalgia, then, for that age of children— so open, simple to address.

Then back here — again sexual insistence I feel, wanting to fuck on and on, the fantasies, again, of Bobbie being fucked by others, an orgy in my own head — till she falls off to sleep, myself too.

In the night, wake several times with terrific dryness, mouth, body — probably the drinking, though have smoked endless amounts of so-called grass. Which continues into the night, i.e., into dreams, so at one point there is very vivid sense of being in what seems a small town, with John Altoon, Bobbie, one or two others I can't now identify or remember. Sense of lane going down to houses, a little like Mallorca — whites and blues, green of trees, grass at edges of cobblestone-like paths. We are talking about impending bust, there's been word of it — waiting, in half-sense, for arrival of police. We expect them to come in one or two cars, probably black, to get out and 'look around.' We anticipate being object of their curiosity, like they say. But have, somehow, a very desultory sense of any impending hang-up, rather, it's something we should pay attention to, but since it isn't now the case, hasn't 'got here' yet, it's hard to do anything. Too, sense of waste somehow in getting rid of the pot before there is literal occasion — however hopeful that obviously is, which, in dream, is also part of our thinking. Then John, first in conversation with Bobbie, apropos her work, talking of senses of painting. Looking then at drawings he's been doing, sense of looking at them right then and there, in the open — a great portfolio, call it, of them, in large dimensions he worked with — great boards, etc. And insistence, his, from time to time, *that's pencil* — which at first I'm confused by, and then see he means it's done of a piece, so to speak, all at once — which he must relate to working in pencil. And one with various trees, one, in particular, dead center, he points to and says, *that's sincerity* — which I take as meaning, that's as much tree as was possible to realize, there, that's all of it, all at once, all I see. And it is — i.e., is crazily intensive seeing, and all *at once*. He speaks of fact he does not work comfortably in 'accumulating' the image, has to be 'all at once'. He is so present, in the dream, it becomes for me like other times I remember talking with him, and what measure of things then came of it continuingly. I see why paint was always (or in some ways) hang-up for him, too slow for what he was doing. As times in Mallorca he was mixing pigments as he worked, finally just dumping turpentine on piles of dry pigment, not even looking so intent he was on the canvas.

My aunt — goodbye. Also John. She had written poem for George Washington's birthday, for paper — would have been printed two days after. She had that 'thing to do.'

SOMETHING PROPOSED in time and space — then, as you'd say — but not as consequence, rather a point of time. But *time* and *space* may well be subjective impressions, like they say. And why not. Speaking of the several 'I/s' so to speak, the habit of saying, what did you think you were, and I answers. Phil Whalen's poem, "Self Portrait In Another Direction" — was an instruction of that time. The layers, but more, the place of where one is, in what constituted, etc.

All of that — tired, a little, against some drag, insistent, of having to get somewhere. Not here. Only included in the action, nothing elsewise 'to be'. It was to be some accumulated so-called 'record' — 'some of my time . . . . '

How to know it. Most real measure now in mind is the saw which the Ainsworths had hanging on the wall in their kitchen in North Lisbon, New Hampshire, of the father, dead by that time — the one he'd made and used. The way such saws were made — first, finding the specific wood for the frame, letting it season, soaking it to get the arch, shaping with knife, etc. Then the saw blade, filed from steel band. The saw become specific to the man using it. Is that sentimental. Going by motels — would there be any use in knowing the specific lives have been lived in them. Or suburbs. Or any such generalization. As against the abandoned cellar holes in woods in New Hampshire, up roads themselves no longer in use. One had sense of the lives that had been there. Or sites of Indian pueblos — a specific locus, a situation that must have been more than coincident.

Two senses, really — the so-called 'individual' and the species group. This is for your own good. Bigger than both of us. But *I* like it. Back and forth, in some endless interchange, apparently (but of no actual?) necessity. The consciousness *thinks* it has experience of this or that. Conceptualizes. Like Alpert's note of the ratio between conceptual units and the content admissible in perception, something like 1 to 20,000 per second. Itself a somewhat unwieldy 'idea'.

Going to sleep. Waking up. Moving. Waking with stomach ache, sudden premonition of death — probably echo of the past weeks and fear of one's own 'time'. What would it be like. Nothing much — certainly nothing you can live in. Aunt's apparent tiredness. Doctor's sense, she didn't want to try to continue living. Better — she knew what she didn't want to do anymore. Arrangements within self, rapport with the surrounding. Keep it moving. Can *thinking* be prior to action, *is* an action, etc. Never felt one would or could think of something previous to its 'circumstances' and/or recognition. Couldn't somehow 'get ahead' of it. Always in situation of 'seeing it' now that 'it's' there.

Go to sleep. Different situation. Time to, go to, sleep. Time to wake up. No time, moving along — no sense of it, no concern. Time enough. But she got caught in it. Whoever she was. Get it over with. Can't wait for this to happen forever. Nor need you. 'Relax and die. Be born! Be born!' How to get somewhere without trying, and *where* is somewhere, etc.

In airport in Denver, lined up with people, about eight in the evening, to take plane to Salt Lake—our category is clear enough, we are going somewhere, for various reasons, in various condition of age, income, etc., in various experience. But all, or genetically all, with eyes, ears, nose and throat. Etc. Tired of dying. Wanted only a trace. A sense of deer tracks, or rabbit — out there, in the snow. Sentimental — thought full of feeling. Welcome, stranger! Come in the door with bag in hand, smiling. Anyone. Anywhere.

Sun's intensity at the window much like the day it all began. Crazy washed-out red, not a pink — but a white red. Must be seven-thirty or so, the day beginning, the kids now off to school and Bobbie returned to bed. Quite quiet — but for stoves cracking, as they light or cool. Hum, it must be, from the refrigerator in the kitchen. Now light of lamp looks very white as other light to the left floods the table . . . .

Had thought of sending, messages of a sort, information from whatever system it is that one is, *keep sending* — Burroughs' 'back to base . . . . ' No 'over and out' as yet, no completion finally of anything. No rest in it, no shape certainly, nothing to do but be doing it. Image of lone telegraph operator, da da dee, da da. Through the long night, so-called. The train roaring toward the trestle, god knows in what hopeless condition, the sagging etceteras. Will help arrive in time.

No help either. Image of person with carefully balanced bunch of packages, another says, oh, let me help you, moves to do so, and because his enthusiasm, or some benighted sense of what he's about to be able to do, makes him unable to recognize what the kingpin of the whole mess is, he so shifts it, in grabbing, the whole bit falls to the ground. Instantly.

Someone saying, someone in Southern Methodist University no less, *The Finger* is too loose. How's that for surrealism by the dozen. Myself was another man, in another country. Or better, that kind of address, years later, of, sir, your son is stepping on our daughter. Get him off. Not possible in that all the skin changes, every seven years — no relative of mine. Law of eternal transcendence.

Back to base. In closing moments already clear in night's dream, a bicycle of some order, now faded, something about some people, a sense of turning occasion. Down the hill.

What the fuck do they think it is. For ages hence? "No thought, of it, but such, pleasure, all women, must be in her, as you." It's clear enough. I do keep looking, in that sense. Out. In. God knows why except that nagging sense of responsibility is somehow still adamant.

So explain myself, to myself. For that you couldn't be blamed, but in other respects, or literally this one, you did not perform in agreement with either your intentions or your stated obligations. But *how* — i.e., dead, does that still 'obligate'? *Outside,* the quotation mark? Was my father, like they say, a deadbeat? He was dead without question. Was that wrong. Now son makes deathly silence, in return, as though he were the tradition somehow of that deadening silence. Retribution of some order one hadn't given a thought to. They won't speak to me either way. In time. But 'myself' am system of an endlessly proliferating consequence. At least I won't live to see the end of it, any more than did Philip, the elder of my two half-brothers, dead of some cause, and Tom, the younger, now with a store in Miami Beach somewhere. How did they know about it — when they started off in Watertown, Massachusetts. What was the 'hidden factor' then. No, they, at least the older, would 'rather be right' than 'wrong' and no doubt was, all his life. At least it was his without question — it never came this far.

So of course there was an end to it, even as it began. That's what's always known — you feel it even as you feel anything, beginning, you have that uncanny, under sense, it will end, I can feel it, the wind, already, drops a little, a waver, something clear enough. But that hardly makes one not want to go, so I always have and will, etc. It's nothing new, wanting to be included.

In London **2**

"But what to do? and
What to do next?"
W.C. Williams,
A Voyage to Pagany

THAT DAY
in an oak tree —
fall's way
comes here.

.

Interrupt-
ions.

.

The room's spaces make the place
of the two persons' sitting seem
years across. One might accept
the "place" of one moving off as
in films a double image permits that separation to be realized.

.

Fire the
half burnt
log, burning,
lies on.

.

Waked to past now dream
of previous place was about to
get all the confusions at last
resolved when he then woke up.

.

What is the
day of the
year we
sit in with
such fear.

WE'LL DIE
soon enough,
and be dead —

whence the whole
system
will fade from my head —

"but why the
tort-
ure . . ." as if

another circumstance
were forever
at hand.
     .

Thinking of dying
à la Huxley on
acid so that
the beatific smile his
wife reported
was effect possibly
of the splendor of
all *possible* experience?

Or else, possibly,
the brain cells,
the whole organism,
exploding, im-
ploding, upon
itself, a galaxy
of light, energy,

forever more.

.

Die. Dead,
come alive.

SIGN

What you know of me —
pale water.
The wind moves

that scattered cloud.
The shimmer of the air,
the sunlight

are perfect
in the mind,
the body.

PACING AS with some consequent
expectance, viz — "look out" —
the expected sequence then waited for.

.

Come fly with me — like,
out of your mind is
no simile, no mere
description — what "mere,"
mare, mère, mother —
"here then," is what you want.

·

Emily — simile.
What are you
staring at?

·

I wanted to find something
worthy of respect — like
my family, any one one knows.

·

What are you crossing all
those out for. A silence lasting
from then on . . .

·

Those out for.
From then on.

Round and round
all the corners.

Love —
let it

Out,
open up

Very,
very *voraciously* —

Everywhere.
everyone.

BOBBIE

"Every one
having the two."

GET IT anyway
you can but first of all
eat it.

TIME TO GO
back where you
were going.

"DICKY THE Stick" —
a stick.

THE EDGE

Place it,
make the space

of it. Yellow,
that was a time.

He saw the stain of love
was upon the world,

a selvage, a faint
afteredge of color fading

at the edge of the world,
the edge beyond that edge.

YOU THINK in the circle
round the whole.

NOW THERE is
still something.

LITTLE TIME —
AND PLACE

You don't say
it is no
answer — you

don't say
it is no
answer.
  •

After and after
round and around.

THE SO-CALLED poet of love
is not so much silent as absorbed.
He ponders. He sits on
the hill looking over . . .

·

A day late —
your love was
still there.

·

Little bits
of it.

·

They are useful
people.

·

No sense one
should be different.

DEAD IN the year —
forms make friends.

"FINE CHINA.
A dollar twenty-nine."

IN THE
mouth — a
hand.

·

Hair is a
long thing

hanging
off.

    •

Out the door

the
ass is

a
way.

    •.

Sitting —
shitting.

    •

Fine manners,
weather,
cars and
people.

    •

No air is
in this
room but
the sounds
occupy all
the space.

RIPPLING EYELIDS
with glister of moisture —

Long time no see.

THE TEACHINGS

of my grandmother
who at over eighty
went west from West Acton,
to see a long lost son named
Archie — by Greyhound, my
other uncle, Hap, got the *Globe*
to photograph her, and us —
came back from Riverside, California,
where Archie was — he'd left
at eighteen — and he'd tried,
she told us, to teach her
religion, "at her age" — "as
much a fool as ever" — and
she never spoke of him again.

DREARY, HEAVY
accumulation
of guilts, debts —
all in the head.
        .

A wind I can
hear outside shifts
the mind, day, eye's
center. A kind.

KIKI

World in a

plastic octa-
gon from a
most perspica-
cious daughter.

A WALL

for Tom

Afternoon lengthens like sunlight
also shrinking as the day comes
to its end in the flickering light.

The leaves make it like that,
the wind moves them, the trees
tower so high above the room's space.

I had walked into a wall, not
through but against it, felt my
shoulder hit its literal hardness.

Sunday. Nothing to worship but
myself, my own body and those
related — my wife, my children, my friends —

but outside, light, it grows long,
lengthens. This world of such changes,
nothing stable but in that motion.

Oh spaces. Dance. Make happiness.
Make the simple the changing —
a little ode to much hopefulness.

ALL AROUND
the town
he walked.

THE MEN in my life were
three in number, a
father, uncle, grand-

father — and with that
father an interchangeable
other — the *Man* — whom

to score with, scream at.
The *wind* rises in a
fucking, endless volume.

NEITHER SADNESS nor desire
seems the edge: this precipice.

DELIGHT DANCES,
everything works.

HOW WISE age is —
how desirous!

LOVE'S FAINT trace . . .

THE SMELL of stale air
in this cramped room.
One sits. The shit falls
below the seat into water.

YOU HAVE nor face nor hands
nor eyes nor head either.

IN LONDON
> *for Bettina*

Homage to Bly & Lorca
***

"I'm going home to Boston
by God"

.

Signs
***

(red)

EXIT
EXIT
EXIT
EXIT

.

(Cards)

Question —
where do you get a pencil.
Answer.
***

.

(for Jim Dine)

most common simple
address words everything
in one clear call to me.

•

("Small Dreams")

Scaffolding comes up the side of the building, pipes,
men putting them there. Faces, in, past one block of windows, then
as I'm up in the bathroom, they appear there too.

•

Ted
is ready.
The bell
rings.

•

Small dreams of home.
Small of home dreams.
Dreams of small home.
Home small dreams of.

•

I love you happily
ever after.

•

(Homesick, etc.)

There is a land
far, far away
and I will go there
every day.

•

12:30 (Read as Twelve Thirty)

(Berrigan
Sleeps on)

.

Voices on the phone, over it — wires? Pulsations. Lovely
one of young woman. Very soft and pleasant. Thinking of
Chamberlain and Ultra Violet — "talking the night away."
Fuck MacCluhan — or how the hell you spell it — and/or teeter-
ing fall, the teething ring, "The Mother of Us All" — *for*
Bob. Call me up. "Don't Bring Me Down . . ."

.

Variance of emotional occasion in English voices — for myself,
American, etc. Therefore awkward at times "to know where one
is." In contrast to Val's Welsh accent — the congruence with
one's own, Massachusetts. Not that they "sound alike" — but
somehow do agree.

.

"London
Postal Area
A-D"

.

Posterior possibilities —
Fuck 'em.

.

"It's 2 hrs. 19 mins. from London
in the train to beautiful country."

"EAT ME"
The favorite delicious dates.

·

Girls
Girls
Girls
Girls

2 X 2

·

Some guy now here inside wandering around with ladder and
bucket. Meanwhile the scaffolding being built outside goes
on and on, more secure.

·

Like German's poem I once translated, something about "when
I kissed you, a beam came through the room. When I picked
you flowers, they took the whole house away." Sort of an
ultimate hard-luck story.

·

Lovely roofs outside.
Some of the best roofs in London.

·

Surrounded
by bad art.

·

I get
a lot
of writing
done —

"You Americans."

·

H — will pirate primary edition of Wms' *Spring and All*, i.e.,
it's all there. Check for Whitman's *An American Primer* —
long time out of print. Wish he'd reprint as Chas apparently
suggests Gorki's *Reminiscences of Tolstoi* [now learn it's
been in paperback for some years]. Wish I were home at this
precise moment — the sun coming in those windows. The sounds
of the house, birds too. Wish I were in bed with Bobbie, just
waking up.

·

Wish I were an apple seed
and had John what's-his-name
to plant me.

·

Her strict eye,
her lovely voice.

·

Così fan tutte.
So machin's alle.

·

Wigmore
dry gin
kid.

·

Wish Joan Baez was here
singing "Tears of Rage" in my ear.

Wish I was Bob Dylan —
he's got a subtle mind.

·

I keep coming —
I keep combing my hair.

.

Peter Grimes
Disraeli Gears

.

That tidy habit of sound
relations — must be in the
very works,* like.

———————

*Words work
the author of many pieces

.

Wish could snap pix in
mind forever of roofs out
window. Print on endurable paper, etc.

.

With delight he realized
his shirts would last him.

.

I'll get home in 'em.

.

The song of such energy
invites me. The song

of

THERE IS a space
of trees —

long since, all
there —

SO BIG

The night's eye
he could say
blandly.

A
word goes
forward —

hands down. She
sleeps beside
him, is

elsewhere. The
movie goes on,
the people

hurt each other.
Now say to her,
love is all.

SWEET, SAD
nostalgia —
walking

by on the
beach a
kid in two

piece bathing
suit of awful
color, girl

with small
breasts, furtive,
half-terrified

a man who
might have been
screaming, a

woman, more
lush, huge, somewhat
fallen

breasts. Waves
coming in as
the tide

goes out, either York Beach,
Maine,
1937 or else

waking, kicking at
the water, the
sand between my toes.

        •

Let me see what you're looking at,
behind you, up close, my head pressed

against you, let me look at what
it is you are seeing, all by yourself.

        •

Echoes — what
air trembles to
sound out like
waves one watches.

I DON'T HATE you lately,
nor do I think to
hate you

lately. Nor then nor now —
lately — no
hate — for me,

for you.

WAY

The walls constituting our
access to the property —

then the path through it,
the walls of that access.

LOOKING FOR a way
the feet find it.

If mistaken, the
hands were not.

Ears hear. Eyes
see everything.

The mind only
takes its time.

BLESSÉD WATER, blesséd man . . .

How long to find you,
how long looking at what is inevitable?

SOUP
   for Mike and Joanne

Trembling
with delight —
mind takes forms

from faces,
finds
happiness

delicious . . .

PEOPLE WITHOUT their own scene
lean.

TWO TIMES

Image
docteur

ee-maj
dok-turr

That's a beautiful coat.

"YOUR WISH came true

to my surprise."

I WANT TO fuck you
from two to four

endlessly
the possibility

I want to
fuck you
        •

Charmed
by his own reward.
        •

A trembling now
throughout.
        •

I am here.

THINKING

Had not
thought
of it . . .
      •

Had nor thought
nor vacancy —

a space
between. Linkage:

the system, the
one after. another —

Though the words
agree? Though

the sounds
sound. The sea,

the woods, *those*
echoing hills . . .

    •

Even in a wood
they stood —

even without sound
they are around.

Here and there, and
everywhere.

    •

All you people
know everything!

All you know you know.
Hence nothing else to?

— Laugh at
that dichotomy.

E.g., the one again
from another one.

Hold it —
to unfold it open.

    •

He wants to sit down
on a chair

he holds in the air
by putting it there.

He wants to sleep in a bed
he keeps in his head.

THE DAY was gathered on waking
into a misty greyness. All the air
was muffled with it, the colors
faded. Not simply then alone —

the house despite its size is full
with us — but an insistent restless
sense of nowhere enough to be
despite the family, the fact of us.

What does one want — more, what
do I say I want. Words give
me sense of something. Days I find
had use for me, how else one thought.

But the nagging, the dripping
weather . . . All the accumulation,
boxes of things piled up the grey
seems to cover, all the insistent junk.

One comes to a place he had not thought to,
looks ahead to whatever,
feels nothing lost but himself.

LOOK

Doesn't he *see*
in the tree
something of *me?*

Or there
wears
no clothes

at all. He
wants
to go

home, *home* —
he wants
to go home.

I WAS NEVER SO upset
as when last I met

another idiot walking by
with much the same preoccupations as I.

FALLING DOWNHILL —
A ball
That falls
And so
Keeps up with itself.

THE MESSAGE

He was wise,
they said,
in being dead.
Nothing more could be said —

But that incredible
idealism, the blur
of the language, how
it says nothing.

Nothing more than that
will do, all
people are
susceptible after all.

FALL

Again you
feel the air
be light a
smoke would
burn in.

Leaves, leaves,
the hill we
drive up over-
hung with leaves,
the trees all covered.

It is funny — strange — to see the young
swirl — leaves, they might be
said to be, in a current of our own.

The limp gestures of older persons,
the hands unable to hold them, all
the world in a flaccid attentiveness —

Now it is fall, and one must yield
again to the end of a cycle, call
it *spring*, and its endless instances.

You will never be here
again, you will never

see again what you now see —
you, the euphemistic

I speaks always, always
wanting a you to be *here*.

    •

How the I
speaks to
you —
over hills.

Continuing forward with a trembling
slipshod insistent sense of affection —
the privileges of vacations, the houses
they have stayed in, the past,

the present, the faces he sees
sometimes before him, the all-
too-suspended times something
less pleasant has proved the case —

his mother's, his sister's, face,
his hands, the outsized now
lower part of his left thumb
from an accident, in Gloucester, last summer —

"Where are all the swallows gone . . . "
as if it were a song he wanted
to remember, had written down to
place among the other things along

a road in summer, such nostalgia,
such airs the summer wears. The grasses
blow and to and fro must walk
all the *things* of life about which one talked.

PERSONS
            for Charles

That this wondering two-footed
notion of abeyance should
think to move and have
come to her and to him
a *nature* and a *place*.

    •

Throw out the *water* — let the land
sit up on it — or in it —

be the wake which forms
at the back of the boat from
all the odds and ends of things.

.

Name the name again, play that
song again. Let the woods roar
in echo again. There is *sun*
as quality of *up* as well as
light fades in the evening, always.

DYING

If we are to exist,
a *we* of an imagination of
more than one, a

veritable multiplicity!
What a day
it is — what

one of many
days and many people,
who live here.

You may bring it
in now
to me. That,

one says, is
the multiplicity —
dying.

"DO YOU THINK ..."

Do you think that if
you once do what you want
to do you will want not to do it.

Do you think that if
there's an apple on the table
and somebody eats it, it
won't be there anymore.

Do you think that if
two people are in love with one another,
one or the other has got to be
less in love than the other at
some point in the otherwise happy relationship.

Do you think that if
you once take a breath, you're by
that committed to taking the next one
and so on until the very process of
breathing's an endlessly expanding need
almost of its own necessity forever.

Do you think that if
no one knows then whatever
it is, no one will know and
that will be the case, like
they say, for an indefinite
period of time if such time
can have a qualification of such time.

Do you know anyone,
really. Have you been, really,
much alone. Are you lonely,
now, for example. Does anything
really matter to you, really, or
has anything mattered. Does each
thing tend to be there, and then not
to be there, just as if that were it.

Do you think that if
I said, *I love you*, or anyone
said it, or you did. Do you
think that if you had all
such decisions to make and could
make them. Do you think that
if you did. That you really
would have to think it all into
reality, that world, each time, new.

MARY'S FANCY

The world pours in
on wings of song.
The radio says
whatever told to

but in mind, air
of another kind,
it holds a place
in the air's space.

Sounds now are
so various, a pig,
goat's bleat. The
burros somewhere.

The air hums, tick
of a watch, motor's
blur outside, a sequent
birds' tweeting. All

the ambient movement
neither seen nor
felt but endlessly,
endlessly heard.

TWO

Holding
for one
instant this
moment —

    •

In mind, in
other places.

THE WALL
one's up against,
the flesh turned stone —

Mind's eye
was memory's
as well as all

those things
that happened. The days
passing, sun

rose and set.
The mind
delighted, else

was tired
of all the flutter
and grew quiet.

The body sometimes
followed,
sometimes led.

There is
or was
no separation

ever, save only
in the head
that knows all.

QUICK TALK
their speech —

will mother
live longer.

will anything
be again here

whatever
it was?

A TESTAMENT

1

We resolve to think of ourselves,
insofar as one of us can so speak

of the other, as involved with
a necessary system, of age and its

factors. We will not be otherwise
than what we are. Our skin

growing more wrinkled, our hair
grey, will not be other than that.

We will laugh, smile, on provocation.
No hysterics shall obtain. We will

love perhaps in other modes but the
yearning, at least my own, will not

grow less, and as I sit now writing this,
a sense of time passing surely,

but with nothing of itself to say,
opaque as the night, dense, always there.

2

Not being dumb
I won't be nor you

either, I think. Not
resistance but no

less than everything,
a rage to keep

even in all respects.
The crickets' humming,

the longer intervals
of other insect

sounds, the birds,
tree toads — al-

ready the ear
has come to hear,

won't accept less.
Say that *I* is

the accumulation
of *my* virtues — breath

lasts, some simile
of water

slopping
to and fro.

3

When they
come to get me,
I'll

give them
you instead —
ashamed,

even trembling
in that fear
of love's

insistences.
But its generosity
will know

I don't go
easily
dragging you after.

HARRY

You're sucking
for a bruise
we used to say.

THE DEATH of
one is
none.

The death of
one is
many.

THE ACT OF LOVE
          for Bobbie

Whatever constitutes
the act of love,
save physical

encounter, you are
dear to me,
not value as

with banks —
but a meaning self-
sufficient, dry

at times as sand,
or else the trees,
dripping with

rain. How shall
one, this so-
called person,

say it? He
loves, his mind
is occupied, his

hands move
writing words
which come

into his head.
Now here,
the day surrounds

this man
and woman
sitting a small

distance apart.
Love will not
solve it — but

draws closer,
always, makes
the moisture of their

mouths and bodies
actively
engage. If I

wanted
a dirty picture,
would it always

be of a
woman straddled?
Yes

and no, these
are true opposites,
a you and me

of non-
sense,
for our love.

Now, one
says, the wind
lifts, the sky

is very blue, the
water just
beyond me makes

its lovely sounds.
How *dear*
you are

to me, how love-
ly all your
body *is*, how

all these
senses do
commingle, so

that in your very
arms I still
can think of you.

TIME

Moment to
moment the
body seems

to me to
be there: a
catch of

air, pattern
of space — Let's
walk today

all the way
to the beach,
let's think

of where we'll be
in two years'
time, of where

we *were*. Let
the days go.
Each moment is

of such paradoxical
definition — a
waterfall that would

flow backward
if it could. It
can? My time,

one thinks,
is drawing to
some close. This

feeling comes
and goes. No
measure ever serves

enough, enough —
so "finish it"
gets done, alone.

THE PROBLEM

He can say, I am
watching a boat tug
at its mooring, a small

rowboat. It is almost
three in the
afternoon. Myself

and my wife are
sitting on the porch
of a house in Grand-

Case, Saint Martin,
French West Indies —
and he says it.

THE TIGER

Today we saw a tiger
with two heads come
bounding out of the

forest by the corner of
Main and Bailey. We
were not afraid. The

war had stopped fifteen
minutes previous, we
had stopped in a bar

to celebrate, but now
stood, transfixed,
by another fear.

THE BIRDS

for Jane and Stan Brakhage

I'll miss the small birds that come
for the sugar you put out
and the bread crumbs. They've

made the edge of the sea domestic
and, as I am, I welcome that.
Nights my head seemed twisted

with dreams and the sea wash,
I let it all come quiet, waking,
counting familiar thoughts and objects.

Here to rest, like they say, I best
liked walking along the beach
past the town till one reached

the other one, around the corner
of rock and small trees. It was
clear, and often empty, and

peaceful. Those lovely ungainly
pelicans fished there, dropping
like rocks, with grace, from the air,

headfirst, then sat on the water,
letting the pouch of their beaks
grow thin again, then swallowing

whatever they'd caught. The birds,
no matter they're not of our kind,
seem most like us here. I want

to go where they go, in a way, if
a small and common one. I want
to ride that air which makes the sea

seem down there, not the element
in which one thrashes to come up.
I love water, I *love* water —

but I also love air, and fire.

ON VACATION

Things seem empty
on vacation if the labors
have not been physical,

if tedium was rather
a daily knot, a continuum,
if satisfaction was almost

placid. On Sundays the restlessness
grows, on weekends, on
months of vacation myself grows

vacuous. Taking walks, swimming,
drinking, I am always afraid
of having more. Hence a true

Puritan, I shall never rest from my labors
until all rest with me, until I am
driven by that density home.

SOUNDS

Some awful
grating sound
as if some monstrous
nose were being blown.

    •

Yuketeh, yuketeh —
moves slow through the water.

    •

Velvet purr,
resting —

   .

Slosh, slush,
longer wash
of it. Con-
verses.

   .

Tseet, tseet —
then chatter,
all the way home.

MOMENT

Whether to *use* time, or to *kill* time, either
still preys on my mind.

One's come now to the graveyard,
where the bones of the dead are.

All roads *have* come
here, truly common —

except the body is moved,
still, to some other use.

AN ILLNESS

The senses of one's
life begin
to fade. Rather,

I ask, who is the man
who feels he
thinks he knows.

I had felt
the way accumulated,
coming from that past,

a prospect beckoned, like
the lovely
nineteenth century. Women

one grew up to
then were there.
Even the smallest

illness changes
that. I saw you
stop, a moment.

The hospital
was a pitiful
construct and

a scaffolding upset
all dignity of
entrance, somehow.

But now it's rather
the people I sat with
yesterday. Across from me

a young woman, dark
haired, and in
her eyes much dis-

traction, and fear. The
other one I
remember was also

young, a man, with
lovely eyes, a greyish
blue. He was

struck by what
we were
hearing, a voice,

on a tape, of an
old friend, recently dead.
Have you noticed

the prevalence
of grey blue eyes?
Is it

silly, somehow,
so to see them?
Your breasts

grow softer now
upon their
curious stem. In

bed I yearn
for softness, turning
always to you. Don't,

one wants to cry,
desert me! Have I
studied

all such isolation
just to
be alone?

Robinson Crusoe
is a
favorite book. I thought

it was a true one.
Now I find
I wonder. Now

it changes. Do you
know that line
that speaks of music

fading up a woodland
path? Or is it
a pasture

I have in mind?
I remember pastures
of my childhood but

I will not
bore you with their
boulders and cows.

Rather those smells,
and flowers —
the lady slippers,

all the quiet darkness
of the woods. Where
have I come to,

who is here. What
a sad cry
that seems, and I

reject it. On
and on. And many,
many years, one

thinks, remain.
Tremulous, we
waver, here. We

love all
worlds we
live in.

PEOPLE
                for Arthur Okamura

I knew where they were,
in the woods. My sister
made them little houses.

Possibly she was one,
or had been one
before. They were there,

very small but quick,
if I moved. I
never saw them.

How big is small. What
are we in. Do
these forms of us take shape, then.

Stan told us of the shape
a march makes, in
anger, a sort of small

head, the vanguard, then
a thin neck, and then,
following out, a kind of billowing,

loosely gathered *body*, always
the same. It must be
people seen from above

have forms, take place,
make an insistent pattern,
not suburbs, but the way

they gather in public places,
or, hidden from others,
look one by one, must be

there to see, a record if
nothing more. "In a tree
one may observe the hierarchies

of monkeys," someone says. "On
the higher branches, etc." But
not like that, no, the kids

run, watch the *wave* of them
pass. See the form of their
movement pass, like the wind's.

I love you, I thought,
suddenly. My hands
are talking again. In-

side each finger must
be several men. They
want to talk to me.

On the floor the dog's eye
reflects the world, the people
passing there, before him.

The car holds possibly
six people, comfortably,
though each is many more.

I'll never die or else will
be the myriad people all
were always and must be —

in a flower, in a
hand, in some
passing wind.

     ·

These things
seen from inside, human,
a head, hands

and feet. I can't
begin again to make
more than was made.

You'll see them
as flowers, called
the flower people —

others as rocks,
or silt, some
crystalline or even

a stream of smoke.
Why here at all
— the first question —

no one easily answers,
but they've taken place
over all else. They live

now in everything, as everything.
I keep hearing
their voices, most happily

laughing, but the screaming
is there also. Watch
how they go together.

They are not isolated
but meld into continuous
place, one to one, never alone.

    •

From whatever place
they may have come from,
from under rocks,

that moistness, or the sea,
or else in those
slanting places of darkness,

in the woods, they
are here and ourselves
with them. All

the forms we know,
the designs, the
closed-eye visions of

order — these too they are,
in the skin we
share with them.

If you twist one
even insignificant part
of your body

to another, imagined
situation of where it
might be, you'll

feel the pain of all
such distortion and
the voices will

flood your head with
terror. No thing
you can do can

be otherwise than
these *people*, large
or small, however

you choose to think
them — a drop of
water, glistening

on a grassblade, or
the whole continent,
the whole world of *size*.

.

Some stories begin,
when I was young —
this also. It tells

a truth of things,
of people. There used
to be so many, so

big one's eyes went
up them, like a ladder,
crouched in a wall.

Now grown large, I
sometimes stumble, walk
with no knowledge of

what's under foot.

　　　　·

Some small
echo
at the earth's edge

recalls
these voices,
these small

persistent
movements,
these people,

the circles,
the holes they
made, the

one
multiphasic
direction,

the going,
the coming,
the lives.

I
fails in
the forms

of them, I
want
to go home.

CHRISTMAS: MAY 10, 1970

Flicker
of *this* light
on consciousness — a

light,
light, green
light, green

tree is the
life. Christmas,
for Christ's

sake, god
damn all thieves!
Green, *green* —

light, goes
by in a
flash.

MASSACHUSETTS

What gentle echoes,
half heard sounds
there are around here.

    ·

You place yourself in
such relation, you hear
everything that's said.

Take it or leave it.
Return it to a particular
condition.

Think
slowly. See
the things around you,

taking place.

.

I began wanting a sense
of melody, e.g., following
the tune, became somehow
an image, then several,
and I was watching those things
becoming in front of me.

.

The *you* imagined locates
the response. Like turning
a tv dial. The message,
as one says, is information,
a form of energy. The wisdom
of the ages is "electrical" impulse.

.

Lap of water
to the hand, lifting
up, slaps
the side of the dock —

Darkening air, heavy
feeling in the air.

.

A Plan

On some summer day
when we are far away
and there is impulse and time,
we will talk about all this.

SOMEBODY DIED

What shall we know we don't know,
that we know we know we don't know.

.

The head walks
down the
street with
an umbrella.

.

People
were walking
by.

.

They will think of anything
next, the woman says.

JUNE 6, 1970

We will write a
simple epic of
sly lust, all

the things we
think of will
be there. He,

says, *sand,* she,
a large cup
of something, someone

screams, all over,
the world erupts,
people laugh.

FOR BENNY AND SABINA

So lovely, now, the day
quiets. What one hoped
for is realized. All

one's life has
come to this, all
is here. And it

continues taking place
for a long time.
The day recovers

itself, air feels
a wet, heavy quiet.
Grey, if one could see the sky.

I felt around myself
for something. I could
almost see you in wanting you there.

It's a hard life at times,
thoughtful, very careful
of all it seems to find.

FOR BETSY AND TOM

We are again
walking in a
straight line — feet

fall, footsteps. We
walk! I am
happy, foolish I

stumble on to the next
person, I think
to myself, charming in

the peace she so manifestly
carries with her. All the
children follow us. The

dogs walk also,
with a sort of sedateness.
They think

they think. We
whistle. I want to
love everyone alive!

SONG

You look out and you see people.
You have some reason in mind.
You are there in a real sense.

I used to
think of the
reasons as if I

knew them. My name
is Bob, I'm
friendly. You can't

go home now. This
is a song,
so they say.

FOR ALLEN

Air of heaven sings.
Raspberries ripen. *Air*
is a familiar presence.

See the dog walk
across the street. He
is limping because you are looking.

IRISH

Her cunt lifts on a
velvet couch, red
velvet, the cry of

Ireland. All the people
I've ever known
salute her. My dear

woman, why have you
left here, why are
you unhappy?

SITTING UP to fill pages having written the poem following
"ahead." Allen's sense so echoes for me — those "mind trips"
he gives me the fact and responsibility of. I really at times
have no idea of what would be "right conduct." Reading this
afternoon about 100 pages of his "Indian Journals" — what difference — such detail — such a specific personal *head* — isn't that
mind? Last night the lady, lovely, vigorous, at the "Dunkin
Donuts" no less, who gives me the 2 dozen now to be stale ones —
"abstract"? I think the *act* can never be. We're all, in our
sense of it, fugitives, all "on the way" — *if* we think at all.
Tom, Betsy, Kirsten, Darrell, David, Elizabeth — Sarah and Kate —
and Spot — and Tiger Sam with his toe now given to eternity.
We'll get there.

YOU

Back and forth across
time, lots of things
one needs one's

hand held for. Don't
stumble, in the dark. Keep
walking. This is life.

WALKING THE DOG

The one to one
walking talk
of the dog — the line

of the dog, tail,
hair
of the dog —

trying,
in reality,
to walk:

a *description*, — hey!
see the dog
walk — a

memory of some
poor son of a bitch dog
walking. Walk

all the way, you'll
get there, poor,
poor dog.

ENVOI

Particulars they want,
particulars they
fucking well will

get, love. For openers,
you — the stars
earth revolves about,

the galaxies their in-
struments neglect. I
walk down a road

you make ahead, not
(no negative) there ex-
cept my body finds

it. Love, love,
love, swirls — myriad
insects hum, the

air softens, the night
is *here*. So empty
these days with-

out you, a box
with nothing in it. I
am waiting, you

are coming, so what's
the world but
all of it.

HEAVEN

"I don't want
my tits
particularized" —

five men in
yellow costumes sneak
into the wings.

I know what's
going on in that
biological waiting room.

Peace, brother,
and sister, and
mother, and you guys.

PEACE

Waiting for a bus,
the bus, vehicle gets me
home to something
where dinner

is prepared with care,
love is found in the icebox,
the bed made, the
clock strikes eleven.

Oh love, oh rocks,
of time, oh ashes I
left in the bucket, —
care, care, care, care.

WISDOM

You could go on
talking to an imaginary
person, real flesh
and blood likewise —

and be none the wiser.
Truth is a small
stream one steps over,
wisdom an insistent preoccupation.

ECHO

I'm almost
done, the hour
echoes, what

are those words
I heard, was
it *flower, stream,*

Nashe's, as Allen's
saying it, "Brightness
falls from the air"?

Was I never here?
The hour, the day
I lived some

sense of it?
All wrong? What
was it then

got done? This
life a stepping
up or down

some progress?
Here, here,
the only form

I've known.

TREES

Thighs, *trees* —
you want
a place to stand,
stand on it.

Body, a vacant
hole, winds blow
through it — the
resonance, of experience,

all words are a vi-
bration, head, chest,
trunk, of tree, has
limbs, grows leaves.

PERSON

Gee, I know
a lovely girl,
woman she
calls herself — did

you ever see a
human being plain,
the body so
inclined? Let me

introduce to
myself myself. I am
one of the race.
I speak an English.

FOR ANYBODY

I could climb a mountain
for a view.

    .

If you get sillier
as you get older,
as you get younger,
that's really abstract.

    .

Allen's got me
on the ropes. I
think of them
all around me.

He went around
the world to see it
and it is as he'd say
there to see.

We're friends, blood
for blood. Death if you want,
we'll pay those dues.
I wouldn't assume

his responsibility
in anything I'd say or do
except I love him
and read what he writes.

    ·

I'm really writing
a valentine in
summer, such
a lovely season.

Here in New England
at last, *at last* —
where I was born,
now they tell me.

FOR CHUCK ◇ HINMAN

So big
the *out there:*
if the one
moves, a pink

faint light, *cut*
each of the
four the *same,* they
are the same:
all around.

FOR LEWIS, TO SAY IT

All one knows, and knows
upon the possibility of knowing,
knowing some-

thing, a thing
that, driven, in-
sists upon its

knowledge. The
ice *melts,* the
water re-

forms, as in a
jail, persons
are *corrected.* I

will not
not succeed. That world
to me is *not* possible.

"OH, LOVE . . ."

Oh love, falling —

the words one
tries

to say are
facts, the
steps, the

walk down
place
and time.

ON ACID

And had no actual
hesitancies, always
(flickering) minds'
sensations: here, here, *here**

philo-tro-

bic-port-

a-bil-ity?

End, end, end, end, end, end

Next? Next who/ who/ they we

          for she me

_____
*or there?   is not we'll

          be . . . . .

PAY

Walking down a
walk, a stone
sees, *assizes*, sizes,

taxes, form
forms. It
says, it is

here — dull,
the de-
scription, it

never seizes,
ever says
enough.

"FOR SOME WEEKS . . . "
for Kirsten

For some weeks
now, caught in my
own complexities, I'd

been thinking
of you, first as
to have your

first child, then
(since not to) as
a woman now

entirely. My
own life, I
thought, this curious

space suit one
lives in, becomes
insistent also.

Think
of Andean flutes
filling the room

with mountains no less!
Dancing, you can
see the goats above you.

Or is it water,
as ever, one feels the
flooding of?

"Liquid notes" —
passion so articulately
carefree, as last.

I've been eating
too much. At times
I feel my stomach

will burst into the room.
My eye seems
to blur at close print.

Pieces
fall away dis-
closing another place.

These faces,
younger, a letter
from someone unknown,

collect much as
whatever would
falling off.

My mother comes
to visit soon. This
part of the country,

New England,
is most her home —
in ways not mine.

I remember
sitting in my sister's
dining-room in Berkeley

with you both
either side — a
warm and open

sunlit day. Possibly
we'll both wander
a long way.

When you first
left home, I had
fears — now

pride fills me,
a man with
a daughter a woman.

Happiness to you,
bless the world
you're given.

HUNGER

He knows
the hunger, walking
in that stiff-legged fashion.

She
knows the hunger,
all her body keeps

telling you you
are not
her. It is

here, I saw
it here. Where
are the people.

Try to
shut me up,
I said, keep

pushing you'll
get it, he,
or someone, said.

I have been,
I *was*, I
am, also.

Jesus Christ, another
one we
got to put up with —

people, and
people, and people,
and people — trees

on Michigan Ave — as
photographed by Harry
Callahan — *trees*,

"I think
that I
will never

see — "
I want some-
thing to eat and

trees — drink
water, places, a
tree in

the hole. We have
to leave

now.

RAIN

Things one sees through
a blurred sheet of glass,
that figures, predestined,

conditions of thought.
                    .

Things seen through
plastic, rain sheets,
trees blowing in a blurred
steady sheet of vision.
                    .

Raining, trees blow,
limbs flutter, leaves
wet with the insistent
rain, all over, everywhere.
                    .

Harry will write
Mabel on Monday.
The communication
of human desires

flows in an apparently
clear pattern, aftersight,
now they know
for sure what it was.

If it rains, the woods
will not be so dry
and danger averted,
sleep invited.

RAIN (2)

Thoughtful of you, I was
anticipating change in

the usual manner. If the rain

made the day unexpected,
in it I took a place.
But the edge of the room

now blurred, or the window
did, or you, sitting, had
nonetheless moved away.

Why is it an empty house
one moves through, shouting
these names of people there?

DOWN HOME

Water
neither knows
who drinks
it nor
denies.

     .

Come
to the
fair
was true
invitation.

     .

Who has
less in there
being *more*?

.

I, I, I,
chatter.

.

The kid
outside the house
walking.

.

Is hunger
only automatic
appetite?

.

Answers:
all
right.

.

Quick
idea of
here was
the place.

.

Never
again
here.

FOR MARISOL

A little
water
falls.

NIGHT

Needs most
happily mutual,
this given,
that taken,

the board clear,
and the food
reappears as
one after one

the night finds
persons in a
lovely particular
display. Here

is a street, and
now a car seems
to be coming,
the lights

signal approach at
an intersection when
a locked group
beats upon the

locked door an
inextricable tenderness
of one man's
desire to be there.

MOUTHS NUZZ

Mouths nuzz-
ling, "seeking
in blind
love," mouths nuzz-

ling, "seek-
ing in
blind
love . . . "

KID

The kid left
out back waits
for his mother's

face to
reappear
in

a win-
dow,
waving.

A TINY PLACE

Walking down
backward, wall
fall, waters

talk, a
crash, much
sound of

noise, *pa-
tience*, a
tiny place.

     •

(Takes
place)

SMOKE

Again in space,
elsewhere,
displaced as they say,

an envoi
to you, thinking
of you, delaying

direct thought perhaps,
since you aren't
here, weren't more

than substantial the
last sight
of you — why

shouldn't there be
the possibility of many lives,
all lived

as one. I don't know,
I don't, can't,
believe it, want

you there,
here, *be*
with me.

Smoke
comes of burning, lifts
in the air that signal,

fades
away, blown,
taken.

KNOKKE
              for Bobbie

Did you notice all the water
in front of you, and the Magrittes,
both murals and what must be

their initial instance, in that room,
at the Casino, where I guess
I'll speak? Funny, walking,

talking to you, passing these
stubby, curious people, the little
bathhouses, some on cart wheels,

labeled "CÉLINE," "FILIP,"
and so on, seeing as I walk
back here, alone, such a distance

to the west, sun shine on waves,
the wind against me, and fall
already here now. You aren't here,

you may never be
as I've known you
again. It's a long way.

> (Knokke, Belgium, 5:55 P.M., in
> room of Hotel Simoens, 9/4/70)

ECHOES

A sudden
loss of hope,
flutters, the
loss of something
known too well.

ROADS

It may be grubs
and worms and
simple change

make the conversion.
I don't think
anymore with clarity,

myself reportedly,
and known as well,
the center of it,

uglinesses, swarms
of discontent, lack-
lustre feeling in

the days. Nights one
doesn't think of, tries
to feel again

what was the way
which brought us here?
To have come to it alone?

LOVE

Tracking through this
interminable sadness —

like somebody said,
change the record.

MOBILE HOMES

Driving along the coast road
with people picked up in passing,

a Roman elegance describes —
often stoned and with an ease

of a car's working well and
silent companions —

describes what fixtures are,
those destinations, places one

means to come to, detrituses,
decisions, mobile homes.

CURSE

The one

man who will
not fuck me
tonight will

be you.

EPIGRAPH

Lot's wife,
married to chance,
luck's, fortune's
foolish bride.

"BOLINAS AND ME..."
                    for Stan Persky

Bolinas and me.
Believe me.

Roy Kiyooka
not here

says that.
Say this.

The human,
the yearning,

human situation
wanting something to be,

which is.
What's wanted?

Let the man put the gas in
your car, John, e.g.,

complete doing what
you wanted him to.

Have *done* with it?
Ham on rye.

The sea, the drive
along the coast in L.A.

I remember Joanne. I
want to. She's

lovely, one says.
So she is. So

are you too.
Or one. Have

done with it.
You see that

line of rocks out there?
Water, waves, two

dead sea lions,
says Peter. He's

lovely. All of them.
Let's walk down

to the beach, see
the sea, say.

If you love someone,
you'd better believe it,

and/or you could,
could write

that all night,
all right. All wrong.

All — isn't enough.
I want to get going. Here's love.

Drive home, up through the mountains,
dense fog. See the car lights

make way of it. See
the night, all around.

Bleed, into the toilet,
two nights, two days,

away from whatever,
go home, and stay there?

I want to walk around here,
look at the people, pretty,

look at the houses, stop in
the bar, get the mail, get

going again, somewhere.
One, two, three, four.

Husbands and fathers.
Sweet love, sweet love.

The kids come
by on bicycles, the little,

increasingly large
people, in the rain.

The liquor store lights
shine out in the night,

and one is walking, going,
coming, in the night.

Holy place we stand in,
these changes — Thanksgiving,

in the circle of oaks,
the sun going west, a glowing

white yellow through the woods.
To the west all the distance.

Things move. You've come to here
by one thing after another, and are here.

Flat thoughts in recalling
something after. Nostalgic twist

of everything so thought — a
period of thought here.

Hair falling, black tangle,
standing in front of the fire,

love dancing, silent, a figure,
a feeling, felt and moving here.

After all it speaks
less in saying more. It, it —

the hunk of wood is
not burning.

Marriage burns, soars —
all day the roar of it

from the lovely barnspace.
The people, the plenitude of all

in the open clearing, the sunlight, lovely densities. I am

slowly going, coming home. *Let
go, let go of it.* Walking

and walking, dream of those
voices, people again, not

quite audible though I can
see them, colors, forms,

a chatter just back of the ear,
moving toward them, the edge

of the woods. Again and
again and again, how

insistent, this blood one
thinks of as in

the body, these hands,
this face. Bolinas sits on the ground

by the sea, sky
overhead.

SEA

Salt and water,
beach sloped form,
wind and water,
it all comes home.

See days
forward, weeks
on end,
opened again.

Past, west,
backwards
water's wake,
a lot of boats.

BILLFOLD

Piece of me, curiously
attached, you were in
a bar for two days un-
drinking and unthinking,
object of your own worth.

FOR THE GRADUATION:
Bolinas School, June 11, 1971

for Sarah

Pretension has it
you can't
get back
what's gone by.

Yet I don't believe it.
The sky
in this place
stays here

and the sun
comes, or goes
and comes again,
on the same day.

We live in a circle,
older or younger,
we go round
and around on this earth.

I was trying to remember
what it
was like
at your age.